MW01602732

God
SAVED MY
Empty
Life

CARMEL'S GRANDDAUGHTER,
Marlene Aaron

ISBN 979-8-89112-856-9 (Paperback)
ISBN 979-8-89112-857-6 (Digital)

Covenant Books
11661 Hwy 707
Murrells Inlet, SC 29576
www.covenantbooks.com

To my wonderful grandmother, Carmel, for her unconditional love and sacrifice. My memory of you and my love for you has no end. Thank you, my Mamaw, for shaping this grandchild's life.

To my husband, Gary. The love of my life now, always, and forever. How blessed I am to have been loved by you. Gary's life was a life lived in love and kindness.

To mine and Gary's daughters, Stephanie and Stacy. Before you were born, you were wanted. After you were born, we would die for you. Your mother and dad's love for you is everlasting.

To my best friend Carole. Your friendship has been one of my life's finest treasures. Because of your loyal friendship, I am a better person. My friend, I love you infinitely.

To all grandmothers, past, present, and future. To all grandchildren whose lives have been or will be influenced by the love of a grandmother.

GOD SAVED MY EMPTY LIFE

God has a good plan for your life.
He has a blueprint with your name.

Contents

Preface

For if ye forgive men their trespasses, your Heavenly Father will also forgive you. But if ye forgive not men their trespasses, neither will your Father forgive your trespasses.

—Matthew 6:14–15 KJV

The wounds we receive from being abandoned; the unfairness and rejection of others will control our lives if we do not forgive. Forgiveness is letting go and letting in the peace and love of God. A long time ago, I forgave my mother, my dad, and others. In my own way, I love my parents. This book was not meant to disparage or condemn my mother and dad. This book was written from my heart. This book was written to share with you the truth.

Jesus was tortured, and he was abandoned. And yet when he hung on the cross, Jesus asked God to forgive his abusers who were crucifying him. Jesus died and suffered so that we will be forgiven of our sins. Remember this the next time you need to forgive someone who has caused you hurt. Forgiveness is necessary so we can have a good relationship with our Lord and Savior, Jesus Christ. This book wants you to have both a relationship with Jesus Christ and wants you to have a good life complete with faith, love, and purpose.

Acknowledgments

I was born August 27, 1947, to parents who gave me away at six months old. They voluntarily gave me to a poor and soon-widowed grandmother to raise. They never came back for me, and they never contributed to my upbringing.

But I have had and still have a wonderful life. In this book, I recognize and give my love and respect to the people who guided and helped me along my life's journey. The most gratitude and thanks belong to God. God loves me and has favored me with his mercy and grace all through my life. He had a plan for my life. A plan and life better than my wonderful grandmother sacrificed to give and prayed for daily. God is the reason and the giver of my every blessing. He let me know he would never abandon me. He is always present in my life and is still flooding my life with blessings. Thank you, God, for keeping me on track and allowing me to live the plan you designed exclusively for me. Even when I disobeyed and went against your plan, you never left me.

Thank you for saving my soul and for giving me salvation. Thank you for allowing me to know Jesus and know of his love and goodness. Thank you for giving your son, Jesus, his blood on the cross, and for Jesus's resurrection so I could be forgiven of all my sins.

Thank you for a good plan and life filled with so many wonderful people you used to mold me and love me. Thank you for my family, serenity, and health. I will never forget being abandoned; however, thank you for helping me forgive my parents and others.

Thank you for the everlasting relationship I have with you. Thank you for giving me eternal life with you, your son, Jesus, and the people I loved here on earth.

I acknowledge I do not deserve your love and your blessings. Your love is stronger, unconditional, richer, and absolute. Your love is greater than anything this world can offer. Your love endures forever. Thank you for your Word, the Bible, so I can get to know you better every day.

This book was written for you; I have felt God wanted me to write a book about my life. My life is no different from a great many more people. If you were abandoned by one or both parents as a very young child, this book is for you.

I have always been and still am a most seriously humble person. I am embarrassed and uncomfortable making this book all about me. But I had to make it about me to witness to you the good life available to all. This book was written to share two truths. The first and most important truth is knowing Jesus Christ as your savior. If you know Jesus, I hope this book will help to strengthen your relationship with him. If you do not know Jesus, I hope this book will help you yearn for and desire to repent and ask him into your heart, giving you eternal life. The second truth—life for you can be good even though you were abandoned by the people who were supposed to love you the most.

I was abandoned by both parents and left at the mercy of a poor, widowed grandmother, I called my grandmother Mamaw. I will refer to my precious grandmother as Mamaw throughout the book. There were several people in my young life who helped make me who I am today. I will dedicate a chapter to each of them.

I did not have to allow the callous and cruel disregard for me shown by my parents control my destiny. I did not have to allow my rocky and uncertain beginning rob me of a life complete with love and purpose; my life experience will show you life does not have to

xiii

be a narrative of your past hardships growing up. God has a good, purposeful, rewarding plan for your life; ask him to give you direction. Live your life loving, serving, and trusting God and his son, Jesus. You will be in awe of what God can and will do for you.

Introduction

My Mamaw, Carmel; my great-grandfather, Pa; my great-aunt Lottie; my best friend, Carole; her parents, Hazel and Harold, helped me overcome a lot of the pain and loneliness that comes with being given away as an infant. These people were good to me, and they showed this little girl she was loved. There was not much to do in my small hometown of Rosiclare. Therefore, strong, lasting, and endearing relationships were created with each of these individuals. Their steadfast support, teaching, and affection carried me through those childhood years and is still part of me today. Their wise instruction, their life's example resonated with me, and I have been reminded often of their good judgment, opinions, and actions. My life has been a reflection and a production of their profound influence.

Without my Mamaw and the other people I mention, all my life would have been sad and without purpose. God had a plan for my life. He is always at my side, never abandoning me. This book is my life seen through the eyes of God. Even with all the negatives along my life's journey, you will learn all through and at the end of the book about a wonderful life, a life blessed with love, happiness, family, peace, and success. A life held close by God. A life God loved so much he stayed faithful every minute, keeping me on the path, making sure I followed his plan.

This book is about the most influential people in my life. Molding a child's character and preparing them for a good, purposeful life begins when they are young. Childhood is a journey from dependence to independence. The people in this book accepted me and gave me love. They were a guiding compass to my most formative years. I spent a lot of time with each of them. They all had a heavy, strong dominance on my character. Now, I still today remember and suffer from being abandoned as an infant. But I have learned to keep those hurt feelings in perspective. However, without these wonderful people in my life, I might have been broken for all of my time here on earth.

These caring and compassionate people with good hearts were all teachers and trainers, gave love, showed integrity, had strength, and had enormous courage. They were good educators of life's most essential loyalties and devotions. They knew their number one job was developing and nurturing my Christian foundation. This was done by their life's example.

I hope this book will give you hope and assurance you are equal to everyone. I hope you know you are important to God. He desires for you a good life. He has a plan for your life, and on his plan is written your name.

I have been where you are in many ways. I am still held captive by all the pain and hurt caused by being abandoned. Know you hold value, you can be happy, and you can know peace. Your happiness depends on you.

You will read how I had no chance until God put a devoted grandmother, Mamaw, in my life. My childhood was poor and sometimes lonely. Lonely because of the way I was treated by my extended family members, church, and school—all because they considered my life circumstances not to be normal, not common, not popular in Rosiclare during the 1950s and 1960s. This contemptuous attitude freed them to show superiority in my presence. They all exhibited and paraded this superior behavior as to invite attention. I was ignored, excluded, and bullied. I was a shy, quiet, passive child and young adult. They all lacked remorse. The adults insensitive, children gleeful, and all appeared to be entertained by causing me sadness. This would have lingering effects on me. This would cause emotional issues taking years managing.

I will give you the advice my grandmother gave me. You are stronger than you think; hold your head high! NEVER QUIT—NEVER GIVE UP! If you were abandoned by a parent or both parents, I hope you will read this book. If you know of someone who was abandoned by their parent or parents, I hope you will encourage them to read the book. Because you were abandoned as a child you will be treated by some spiteful people with contempt. Give these people no satisfaction in defining your value and your life. Know you are equal to everyone and never settle for less than a good life. Never limit what you have to offer. Everyone should live every day of life choosing to dream of their future and not living the history of their past. If you live in the past, that is an anchor that will firmly attach itself to you. That anchor will keep you from reaching your potential. Living in the past will keep you from a productive, fulfilling, meaningful life of love, promise, and dreams. Always remember your past, but do not live your past.

In a lot of ways, I believe growing up with parents who did not want me made me stronger. I was determined to prove myself to the people I was acquainted growing up who acted and thought I was not their equal. They treated me this way because I was left to be raised by my poor widowed Mamaw. Some people will be cruel if they think you are lower in status and less important. They will cause you to feel incomplete. Don't let them win.

Be strong, be brave, be obedient to God, be positive, believe in yourself, make smart decisions, and never give up on your goal. Get as much education as possible. Get a job, work hard, save your money, and live in faith. The good life can be yours.

God kept his plan for me alive and working. I was born to a life forgotten, alone, unwanted, abandoned, and unloved, a baby born having nobody. An innocent life with no hope and no future, but

God's plan was to place me in the arms of a precious and faithful grandmother. I still have a lot of insecurities. Unfortunately, I still have low self-esteem and feelings of inadequacy. But I have learned to push them to the side as necessary. As an adult, I found love and became a mother and the owner of a successful business.

It took God's love, protection, and holding me close. It took the love, assuredness, and patience of the wonderful people I devote a chapter. It took all of them years to get me to the happy and successful life I experience. God made all these people part of his plan for my life. I do not deserve the blessings God has given me. He has been my constant companion all my life, and I love him and thank him. The love and devotion of Mamaw, Pa, Aunt Lottie, Carole, Hazel, and Harold. The love, kindness, understanding, and support of my husband, Gary. The sole proprietor of a successful independent insurance agency for thirty-three years. But I believe God's greatest plan for my life was to be Stephanie and Stacy's mother. Both girls love Jesus Christ and live in faith. My life would have remained empty, but God had a plan. And God would NEVER QUIT—NEVER GIVE UP.

1

Getting to Know Mother and Dad

This is a book about a baby girl who had no chance of a good life. My parents were living a life of conflict, confusion, aggression, bitterness, destruction, anger, and so on. I would have this kind of life with them. I would have a life without the love and protection of a mother and dad. I was born to parents who considered me an insurmountable obstacle. I was a problem that if kept would interfere with their love for themselves. For them to be happy, they must be free of responsibility and free of me.

Most regrettably, my mother and dad would complete the description of deadbeat parents. They refused to fulfill any of their parental responsibilities. And yes, there are parents who do not care about their biological children. Neither one of my parents ever told me they loved me. I had no relationship with them. They never told me or shared with me anything relative to being their child. They barely acknowledged I existed. I was born with an empty life. I had nobody.

My parents were young when they married. They immediately moved in with my grandparents causing many challenges. My parents brought stress and worry to my elderly grandparents. They gave

1

my grandparents both emotional and physical concerns to endure and suffer through. They brought financial problems to my grandfather. He worked every day in the mines for Alcoa. My dad did not work. My mother was too young to work. They made their home with my grandparents from July 1945 until November 1947.

I was born at my grandparents' house. We all lived with my Mamaw and my Papaw until I was three months old. My parents moved to Waukegan, Illinois, when I was three months of age. They separated when I was six months of age. My dad stayed in Waukegan, Illinois. Mother would drop me off at my grandparents' house, and she would go to Griffin, Indiana. They would never come back for me. I was at my home in Rosiclare with my loving, nurturing grandparents.

My Mamaw Carmel and my Papaw James Anderson would support Mother, Dad, and me until November 1947. Their daughter, my mother, had always been a child out of control. My Papaw, commonly called by his nickname, Burrell, would work and support the family while my dad stayed home and did not work. Papaw never complained. He worked every day with a failing heart. When my parents separated and Mother dropped me off at my grandparents, they took me, and they loved me. This infant grandchild did not have anyone. My grandparents' hearts were broken for me. Papaw with his failing health took me to raise. He and Mamaw never regretted this big responsibility. Sadly, my grandfather passed away when I was twenty-one months old. But Mamaw would finish what they together started. Mamaw thought of me as a blessing. She knew God's plan for her was to love and care for me. And she did.

My life journey had begun. I would see my dad two times, totaling about four hours, until I was nineteen years old. When I was nineteen, I reached out to him. My mother visited Mamaw about three or four times a year. I had no relationship with either parent. When my mother visited, she never acted like a mother. I never had a friendly, emotional, or attached relationship with her. I rarely remember her acknowledging me. She came to visit Mamaw, her mother, and her brother, Uncle Ben. She never thought of me as her child. I was forgotten by both parents.

They contributed nothing to my upbringing. My dad who never came around never knew how my life was progressing. Neither one of my parents gave my grandmother as much as a dime toward my care.

Even with a very rocky start, I have always had a good life. I always had the love of a grandmother. I know children abandoned by parents is a disturbing, fearful experience. This has many adverse effects on the child's mental, emotional, and social development. I know, I have been there my entire life. But we learn from this, and we never allow their neglect to destroy our future and our destiny with happiness. We will not be the victim. We will be the victor. We will overcome and defeat the emotional struggle of absent parent or parents. We will not harbor ill will, deep bitter anger, resentment, or malice. We are going to be happy, and we will be thankful for the blessings we have. We know being happy is a choice and not an occurrence of life. Our parents gave us a bad beginning we were too young to change. But we will not let them ruin our finish. We will strive every day on earth to not be like them. My parents' failure to have human decency, their dereliction of duty to me, did make me stronger. We will be committed to leaving a legacy of hope, promise, and dignity to our family, friends, and every future generation. Our parents' neglect and lack of love has gifted us determination to have a good life. We know our life will be what we make it. Our faith will remain strong. Our life is about the present and the future. It is not about our past. We will stay true to the core values that will lead us to opportunities. Our parents denied us a good beginning to life. However, they will not deny us a good finish. Our life's beginning has made us strong, resolute with an unwavering mindset. We have been given the strength and wings of an eagle. Watch us soar!

Being abandoned by parents will cause many problems. If you are suffering from these problems, I would encourage you to seek medical help. Do not be embarrassed to ask for a doctor's attention. I have not sought professional help, and that has been my decision and my choice. However, I am sure I could have benefited from medical services.

2

Family Is Destroyed— Baby Is Deserted

This book is written in truth, and my words come straight from my heart. It is sometimes very difficult to be honest, direct, critical, and outspoken and not offend someone. We never get anywhere in our life if we do not acknowledge the truth; until we tell ourselves the truth, we will continue with the same mistakes. Truth is power. Nothing can compete with the truth. Truth never changes, and truth never dies. Truth is the foundation upon which every human relationship is built and protected and endures.

You will hear in your lifetime people speak often about how difficult it is to maintain a loving and loyal grasp on a family. My life's observation tells me with definite assurance this is accurate.

I think we would all agree a child needs a family structure. The traditional family structure in America involves two married individuals providing care and stability for their biological offspring. Family structure is defined as a combination of relatives that comprise a family.

Children mostly benefit from family. Family gives them a sense of belonging, love, and acceptance. This has a tremendous bearing on the child's emotional, social, and behavioral development. Children who experience their family's hurtful disruption are at a higher risk of having functional difficulties. This includes depression, anxiety, and academic failure. I experienced all these problems growing up, and I am conscious of the fact that my spirit is still dampened after all these years as a result of the neglect and abandonment of both my parents. Their parental failure was very damaging to my life. I have often wondered why I cannot make friends, why I do not socialize well in crowds or even with one individual. My dad and mother had many friends; they never lacked social acceptance. I went years wondering what was wrong with me. I was and still am, in many circumstances, rejected today. But I have learned that a lot of the fault is not the people I try to connect and be friends with. It is me! And even though I have been given a very fulfilling, happy life, I will always have difficulties because of the actions of my parents.

We expect parents to love their children unconditionally, and I believe most do. When parents make mistakes, we accept them because we long for the love of our mother and dad. But children rejected by parents experience low self-esteem. These children have a negative opinion of their self-worth.

My parents, especially my mother, married very young. Dad was twenty years and six months old, and my mother was two months away from being thirteen years of age. They were married in July 1945, and I was born in August 1947. I have often wondered if it was common for a girl to be married at that young age in 1945. I was their only child.

They began their married life by making their home with my mother's parents. I was born at my grandparents', Mamaw and Papaw's, house. Both parents deserted me at six months old, and they would never come back for me. They each contributed nothing to my care and upbringing. I was left my entire life knowing I was not loved and wanted by the people who were supposed to love me and want me the most. Unfortunately, their behavior is worthy of severe criticism. In small Hardin County, Illinois, everyone knew everyone, and they knew everyone's business too. My parents' flagrant behavior drew attention to their deliberate mistreatment and neglect of me, their child. For some reason, this made me unpopular with adults and children, and it made me unpopular and not accepted by most of my extended family too.

Both my parents willfully and intentionally withheld physical, emotional, and financial support from me. They both passed away with no discussion or explanation of their decision to be separated from their child. They both were young and immature. They were selfish, and neither wanted responsibility. Their behavior was destructive, irresponsible, and did damage to me my entire life. Selfish people create splintered and broken families. Their sense of self-importance and their love for themselves destroy. I suffered emotions of sadness and anger before coming to some acceptance. Even though I had the love and devotion of my Mamaw, great-grandfather, and great-aunt, I still ached with guilt and shame. Little children often feel they are to blame for their parents' abandonment of them. I was weakened through and through. I grew up insecure and showed signs of anxiety. I consistently worried about everything, and this carried over into my adulthood. I was a nervous child and afraid of anticipated day-to-day events. I feared close relationships. Children and adults abandoned by parents can alienate friends, and fear impairs their ability to trust others. I withdrew from people and have feelings that I do not deserve to be loved. Of course, this is not true but expected. I still continue to cope with most all the destructive harms of abandonment. We never get over not being loved and wanted by our parents. Through the years, we learn to cope.

We attempt to figure out ways to deal with and adjust to the emotional damage we have been caused. The damage they did to break our young souls; our spirit will last into our present time. But it will not keep us from having a life of purpose filled with love, peace, and achievement. We are survivors, we have strength, we are courageous, and most of all, we have the love of Jesus. Jesus values your life as much as all others. You are responsible for being happy. It is your state of mind. Jesus gave your life purpose. Hold your head high.

Abandoned girls will most always have few female friends. They probably will feel unworthy, always striving for perfection and acceptance. They will drive and send people away because they fear they are unlikable.

There is great harm done to children because of the selfish actions of their parents. The defaulting negligence of parents' duty to their child causes the child to suffer lifelong mental trauma. The child may have lasting feelings of guilt and self-blame. The parent or parents left the most helpless, vulnerable, and innocent to manage the trauma of feeling less loved, less safe, and less equipped to enjoy a life that is self-satisfying, developing and using possessed potential. Less able to be independent and less capable of acquiring the basic things that are necessary. I have struggled with all the issues and problems I discuss. And the truth is, I still struggle. But I would not and will not let it destroy my life. I know my deadbeat parents were not my fault. I know I am not the only person who was denied the love and care of parents. I believe I am special because of this situation. I believed I had a good future ahead of me. I realize problems and trials help us develop endurance. Endurance strengthens our character, our willpower, our good qualities, and our God-given talent and gifts. What matters is not only we overcome and fix the problems of abandonment but how we fix them. Determination introduces us to humility. We know and learn we are as important as anyone, but we have no more importance than anyone. Humility is the ability to think and act with good judgment. It is the skill to detect right from wrong and lean right. Humility is not thinking less of yourself, but thinking of yourself less. Humility is wisdom.

Marlene's Baby picture.

3

Mother

I will discuss later in this chapter why I think my grandparents allowed my mother to get married so young. This would mean Mother needed to drop out of school and receive little primary education. This usually means life is difficult and her life was always difficult.

My Mamaw and great-aunt Lottie said Mother was always hard-headed even at a very young age. She was always determined to have her own way. She was forever exhibiting willfulness. She was very disrespectful to everyone in our family, and this behavior extended to everyone in her life over the years. I witnessed more than I care to remember Mother's violent and uncontrollable behavior. If she did not get her way, if she felt slighted with attention, and if the conversation was not going her way, there was a brutal verbal scene. She would scream, use swear words, cry, accuse, ridicule, criticize, mock, and slur. It did not matter where she was or who was in attendance. She never showed regret for her many outbursts of rage. In the beginning, my mother was very young and immature and did not want to be burdened with a baby. I do not think she ever wanted to be a mother. Her life was sad, so many wrong decisions. She could not be patient enough to take time to examine her life and get a purpose and a passion.

Mother lived two hours from Rosiclare and visited for the weekend about every three months. Sometimes she would be there less than an hour. She would get mad, have an eruption of a violent venting temper tantrum, and go back home. She was a very jealous individual and never thought of anyone but herself. She would abuse, ridicule, and intimidate her mother, my Mamaw. Mamaw would say nothing for fear my mother would take me home with her. The court gave me to my mother in the divorce. Her relationship with her mother, my Mamaw, was hopeless. The fractures had been constant for so long they were beyond healing. My mother never kept a friendship very long. Her life was sad, bitter, and full of hostility.

She had three failed marriages, but in fairness, the husbands were not quality people. The spotlight must always be on her. She always played the pitiful victim. Her personality was toxic, with much negativity and drama. Family said my grandmother had a sister with a like personality and behavior. Maybe her angry attitude was an inherited instinct. I never witnessed any other family member with this aggression. If anything, they were passive and harmonious most of the time, if that is possible.

I do know my mother and my Mamaw loved each other. Some relationships will not work despite how desperately you want them to. Their relationship remained hostile. They both grieved over Mother's hostile feelings but never had an enduring mother-daughter bond or connection.

My mother was a hard worker and had a good job with the same employer for more than thirty years. She never gave Mamaw anything toward my care. All I ever received from her was a birthday and Christmas gift. My mother could not make herself happy. I think one reason for this was she was impatient, always rushing into decisions. Patience is a virtue. Patience was never welcome in Mother's life.

Mother made lots of friends. Making friends was easy for her, but she could not keep them long. Something about her always meant she would express to them mean comments and criticism. She was rude and cruel. Most people respond to this kind of treatment by detaching themselves from the individual causing them hurt and stress. Her personality was destructive unless she was getting all the attention all of the time. Life is not that way. My mother never recognized life was not intended to be all about her. She always put herself first. All her relationships were difficult and ended terribly.

My mother's life was troubled, melancholy, and sad. A lot of this was caused by her bad decisions. She was empty and confused. I do not believe she experienced love. I don't know if she knew how to love. If only she had let God intervene, her life would have been much different. I believe mothers are the most important people in the universe; all things considered, I think my mother did the right thing by giving me to my grandparents. She realized motherhood was not something she wanted. Her decision to give me away caused me a lot of pain and insecurity. However, the pain and insecurity would have been greater had I made my life with her.

I know my grandparents allowed my mother to be married so young for fear she would become pregnant. She was out of control. She persistently and habitually refused to obey her parents. Her behavior was impulsive, and she never considered the consequences of her actions. She acted on emotion and had no self-restraint. My grandparents were good people. They must have thought there was no other way. Mother was going to do anything she wanted regardless of the damage her decision would inflict on others.

My mother did accept Jesus Christ as her savior. She passed away at the age of ninety.

4

Dad

In a big way, my dad could be more at fault for my abandonment and the mistake of marrying my mother. He was older, twenty years and six months when they married; and Mother was two months away from being thirteen years old. She was a child. I think it is fair to say my dad was extremely selfish and only interested in himself. His actions left me with chronic fear and insecurity that continued still into my adulthood. He was 100 percent absent, no support and no contact. For all my life and still today, I suffer debilitating self-esteem. We never get over being abandoned. We just learn to accept and cope and do our best to minimize. After all these years, a good life, I still continue self-doubt.

My dad had no conscience toward me. He had no blameworthiness of his lack of actions, intentions, or obligation. He did not have the ability or the heart to love me and want to make sure I was cared for. It was obvious, I meant nothing to him. Our conscience is our moral fiber. Dad lacked remorse for inflicting me with many negative issues and problems, complicating my life. My dad was poor in caliber and grade. He was irresponsible, inadequate, and weak toward me, his child.

I do not know a lot of particulars about my dad's life after my parents' divorce. Dad was 100 percent absent from my life. In my first nineteen years of existing, I saw him two times, totaling maybe four hours. The first time he came to see me, I was five and a half years old. Even at that young age, I remember him. His mother had passed away. The next time I saw him was on my thirteenth birthday. I remember that time too. I was having a birthday celebration with my friend Carole. I was enjoying my new twenty-six-inch bicycle my grandmother bought me for my birthday. She purchased the bicycle at the Western Auto store in Rosiclare. It was bought on layaway, meaning she would pay a little on the bike each week until it was paid. Back then, the bike cost $20. That was one week's income for my grandmother. She did the same four families' laundry each week at $5 each for as long as I remember. When I graduated high school, she was still washing and ironing for people.

My dad's father had passed away. Dad came for the funeral and made the decision to see me. It happened it was my birthday. The only times I saw Dad growing up were at the death of his parents. This time I was thirteen years old, and he brought his wife and their three children. It was the first time his children knew they had a half sister. He had kept me a secret. It has always bothered me how my dad could abandon his firstborn, as was my case, and be a dad to his other children by another woman.

Dad was born and raised in Elizabethtown, Illinois. He and his family had the reputation for heavy drinking (beer), and they all partied hard. Their life was all about fun and good times. Responsibility was a word unfamiliar to him, his dad, and some siblings.

When Dad was young, duty, obligation, and commitment might as well have been foreign words. His happy and breezy, carefree ways won him a lot of friends. He was handsome and had a good physique, and many people thought him to have a great personality. Dad was a looker and popular with everyone. In his youth, he would not allow anyone or anything to get in the way of his recreation, entertainment, or his engaging in light-spirited pranks and frolic.

Dad came to Elizabethtown, Illinois, every August to visit his family. His mother and dad lived there until they passed. Several of his siblings and their families lived there too. Elizabethtown is in Hardin County, Illinois, and only three miles from Rosiclare. He came to see me only two occasions growing up, even though he spent every summer vacation in Elizabethtown. As previously mentioned, those two visits I got were at the passing of his parents. I guess death does that to some people. He would continue to visit his family in Elizabethtown every August, but he would never come to see me again. That is how much I meant to him. Three miles away and he could not come see me.

The next time I heard from him, I was nineteen years old. I had graduated school and was working in Jacksonville, Illinois. I took it upon myself to call him and make contact. I guess the reason for this action was curiosity; maybe I wanted to gain knowledge and information, or maybe I just wanted to fill in the blind spot and the gap in my life with him that he caused. Maybe I wanted to show him that I did survive and that he could no longer treat me as being void and nonexistent. More than anything, I wanted to know if he could finally love me. But he could not. He had another family, and I was nowhere in his memory.

After I married, my family made three or four trips to Waukegan to visit him and his family. Dad made us feel welcome. However, by the time I reached out to him at the age of nineteen, he had suffered an accident at his workplace. This accident left him almost deaf. Therefore, we never got to talk or know each other. I don't believe he ever regretted ignoring me. He never wanted anything to do with me. He was escaping personal and financial responsibility. There was never an explanation or an apology for his past wrongs. I also got a strong sense of feeling that he was a man with a very prideful heart.

It would give great difficulty to him to ever say he was sorry and regretted his abandonment of me.

In the divorce, the court gave my dad visitation rights anytime he wanted. Of course, he had no intention of ever exercising them. Mother did not ask for child support. Inevitably she did not get any either. Another bad decision on the part of Mother.

I think my dad changed some as he grew older. He was very likable, a good friend and a good son and brother. And I believe he was a good dad to his other children. Reference me, he was an appalling and contemptible disappointment and failure. Always indifferent, having no interest, no concern, no involvement, and no responsibility. God has an amazing and awesome sense of humor because I have the appearance of looking very much like my dad. I know that was intended. Dad stayed married to the mother of his other three children until his death. Of his three children, only my half brother will have a relationship with me. I have a good rapport with him and his family. He refers to me as his sister. We respect and like each other. His two sisters want nothing to do with me or my family. I am thankful for my half brother for he is the only link to Dad. We never talk of the past. He loves Dad, and I never want that to diminish.

My dad never contributed one thing to my upbringing. I never received a card or a birthday or Christmas gift. I never received a phone call or anything while growing up. He never gave my Mamaw as little as a penny to help support and care for me. He did provide very well for his new family of a wife and their three children. The only thing I ever received from Dad was his name.

Dad became very sick, and his time was running out. Knowing this, my half brother witnessed to Dad many times, asking if he could bring his minister to the hospital to visit. Dad, being the stubborn and prideful person he was, refused his son's offer. My dad had probably never been to church except weddings and funerals. Dad passed away at sixty-three years. To our knowledge, he never accepted Jesus. We are hoping for a miracle before the end of his life.

Mother was verbally abusive to everyone. No person in her company would escape her labeling, scolding, yelling, insulting, intimidating, and ridiculing. Many times this abuse toward others would become physical. She obviously could not or would not control her anger and temper. This proved to be a serious flaw in her character. She blamed everyone for the mistakes made in her life. Her life was sad. I think about her often and so wish her life could have been happy.

Dad had no desire to know what would happen to me. He knew if Mother raised me, my life would be extremely sad and most probably have an unhappy ending. He did not care where his baby girl would call home. He just knew it would not be with him.

Regrettably, we all make mistakes, many mistakes. Some of us seem to attract more mistakes than others, but we are all guilty. Both mother and dad were selfish and self-centered. If they were having a good time, if they were in pursuit of pleasure, if they were in the company of so-called friends, they were happy and life was considered at its best. No regard for anyone except themselves and their gratification and enjoyment.

Dad is in Waukegan, Illinois. Mother is in Griffin, Indiana. I am at home in Rosiclare with Mamaw. My mother and dad are off to a life excluding me with never a thought or care about the child they left behind. My parents invited rejection, scorn, insecurity, and feelings of unworthiness into my young life. Their action and contempt for me would build my character and my strength that would surface in my adult years. Mamaw is making me prepared for joy in the years ahead. Painfully, this transformation of my weakened willpower, self-esteem, determination, and resolve would not take place until I found the love and support of my husband. Today I still suffer all of the above, but I am stronger. I have proved if you work hard, save your money, play by the rules, find a wise mentor, and graduate school, you can have a life of purpose. This is capable of happening to all. Be of good attitude. Have a good opinion of yourself. Hold your head high! NEVER QUIT—NEVER GIVE UP. And most importantly, have Jesus in your life. All this is the advice of Mamaw.

5

Divorce Is Final

I am less than a year old, and the marriage is over. The court gave me to Mother. I have their divorce papers. In 1948, the State of Illinois would grant a divorce in six weeks. I am now one year of age. My mother told a family in Rosiclare they could adopt me. They were a prominent and respected husband and wife. She was unable to conceive children. According to family members, this couple would take me several weekends in a row to bond with this baby girl they hoped to adopt. They would return me to my grandparents' house. Soon the adoption papers were ready for signatures. Mother was in the attorney's office with the couple. The hopeful adoptive parents had signed the adoption papers. However, Mamaw and Uncle Ben cried and begged Mother not to sign. At the last minute, she backed out of the adoption. Mamaw and Uncle Ben promised to help with me. I do not know if my dad had to sign. Divorce and adoption were handled much differently by the courts in 1948. It was Mother's failure to sign papers that put an end to my adoption. Mamaw kept her promise, but Uncle Ben did not.

Mother left again for Griffin, Indiana, and the responsibility of raising me was determined. I would be raised by my wonderful Mamaw and Papaw. But this was not God's plan. Grandfather passed away in May 1949. Mamaw and I went to live with her widowed father and unmarried sister. They became my Pa and my aunt Lottie. Like my grandmother, they would love me and want me. I was never a burden to those old people. They looked at me as a blessing. I was the joy of their lives. Truthfully, I was always a shy, quiet, sweet, polite, and mild-mannered child. I never gave them trouble. Because of my love, respect, and gratitude for them, I never wanted to be a disappointment. I never wanted to cause them heartache, make them sad, or give them worry.

There was never a dirty word spoken, never a display of anger from these three old people. I would be a big responsibility but they did not mind. God kept all of us safe and provided all our needs. He kept those three old people healthy until they had lived out his plan for them. I had graduated school and was ready to strike out on my own. They were sad the day I left for Jacksonville, but they knew there were no job opportunities in Rosiclare. I bought a car after about nine months and visited them every other weekend. At that time, it was the longest nine months of my young life. They were the only family I had ever known. I was handed over, donated to, given away, and disposed of by my parents as a baby. Their actions caused shame, embarrassment, and irreparable injury. Those three elderly people with good hearts and lots of love to give, upon the authority of God, took me to raise. They had no money, no education. But their quality, contribution, conduct, and life achievements can only be given to someone who has the touch of the master's hand. To me, the little girl with no one, they all three were first-class, first-rate, five-star, and top-notch.

> But if any provide not for his own, and specially for those of his own house, he hath denied the faith and is worse than an infidel. (1 Timothy 5:8 KJV)

I have forgiven my mother and dad. This was not easy for me, and it was a lengthy process. The hurt they caused will never leave me; however, God helped me forgive. Holding onto anger and bitterness will inflict us with more suffering, keeping us from having the good life. Forgiveness is healing. Being happy is a choice; being happy is your choice.

6

My Hometown, Rosiclare

I was born and raised in Rosiclare, Illinois. Rosiclare is in Hardin County, Southern Illinois. Hardin County is one of the smallest counties in the state, both in area and population. There are three small towns in Hardin County: Rosiclare, Elizabethtown, and Cave-in-Rock. Elizabethtown is the county seat; however, Rosiclare has always been the most populated. When I was growing up in Rosiclare, the population was somewhere around 2,200 people.

The story has it that the town was named after two daughters of an early French settler. The two girls' names were Rosi and Clare. The town incorporated and received its charter from the state of Illinois in 1874. This means Rosiclare was allowed to have its own elected officials. Rosiclare became a city/town in 1932.

Rosiclare is on the Ohio River. Main Street dead ends into the beautiful Ohio. There is only one way in and one way out of town. Many residents always thought this was one of the reasons Rosiclare did not grow. It was and still is a slow-paced, quiet little town without a lot of excitement and activity. The town's residents are mostly comprised of plain, simple people, relaxed, and calm—free from aggressiveness and anxiety. The people had all the basic and necessary things required but very little of anything more. They did not care about missing out on what some people would call the finer things. The residents' mindset was to create a meaningful and conscious lifestyle that was in line with what they valued most in their life. They were happy to be at home in Rosiclare with their family.

The best way to describe Hardin County and Rosiclare is having beauty. Its uneven ground of bluffs, hills, the Ohio River, valleys, and the winding roads are magnificent. Her natural landscape is extremely beautiful and rare. It is unlike anything you will ever see. Rosiclare is a place with fishing, boating, walking, picnics, hunting, horseback riding, farming, biking, and more. Rosiclare was an idyllic small town. It had the characteristics of outdated, antiquated, and old-fashioned. A little town that still belonged to much earlier time. Rosiclare was a place where almost everyone would be accepted and treated favorably. That was not the case some of the time for me and Mamaw. No matter where you live, where you work, where you go to school, where you go to church, even your family, everywhere some people will show cruel treatment. Misconduct will inevitably be exposed for all to witness. I have no explanation for this except this will always be the nature of some people. Mamaw was immensely poor and raising a grandchild whose parents did not want. She was supporting this child by doing laundry, babysitting, and cleaning homes. This did not work for some of Rosiclare's elitist and some of her considered finest. Even so, the way of life, the southern Illinois dialect, and the humdrum of everyday Rosiclare would put you at ease and give you serenity. Mamaw did not allow the bad behavior of some to concern her.

From Rosiclare's varied groups of residents, I would learn a lot of life's valuable lessons. These life's lessons of knowledge and principles would stay with me for all my life. Many years back or many years forward, I will still call the town of my birth and childhood home. Rosiclare will always own a special place in my heart. Growing up in Rosiclare influenced my life in important ways, contributing greatly to who I am today.

Lead and fluorspar were discovered in Rosiclare around 1843. Eventually, Rosiclare was the site of one of the largest mining operations in the nation. During World War II, the demand for lead and fluorspar was great, and Rosiclare was one of its biggest suppliers. The big "Alcoa," Aluminum Company of America, came to Rosiclare and made her a prosperous little community. Alcoa and fluorspar mining were the life and blood of Rosiclare. Now we were thriving. We always had the good life. But now it was even better. Men came to Rosiclare from all around to work for Alcoa. The men went to work in the mines. The women's primary interest was home and children. Everyone worked in those days. No living off the government like it is now.

They say nothing lasts forever. By the mid-1960s, Alcoa closed its mines in Rosiclare. They had been there for many years. I don't know why they left. Rumor circulated a story of the fluorspar being depleted, making it no longer profitable to stay. Alcoa gave the town residents a good job that enabled them to provide and raise their family. Alcoa was the town's power and energy. Alcoa was Rosiclare's incalculable and enormous gift. When Alcoa left Rosiclare, she instantly and all at once became a town with very limited employment opportunities. Her population today is around one thousand people. There are only a few businesses left to meet the immediate needs of the residents.

Hardin County has rich soil that will grow anything. Good ole Illinois farmland. Lots of farms in Hardin County. My friend Carole and I could walk or ride our bicycles all over town and not be concerned with danger or being accosted by anyone. Residents did not have to lock their doors at night. We could go all night in the summer with windows raised.

Rosiclare does not have much to offer these days. After a child graduates, they would need to leave to find work. Today, most of the young people who stay in Rosiclare will know poverty. There is no future for career or job advancement. However, if they leave, the experience of growing up in Rosiclare will always be on the other side of their mirror, showing her teaching of common sense and good judgment. This will be revealed many times in life. Many industrious people have their roots in Rosiclare. It was a great place to raise a family. It was a great place to raise me.

My hometown was the perfect example of a small town. It had all the characteristics. Good old American values and traditions that have proven over and over to work to everyone's advantage. Rosiclare had charm. There were no strangers. No crime, and everyone felt safe. Small-town low cost of living, no traffic, and no pollution to name a few. Almost 100 percent of families stayed together. Quality of life for most everyone was considered good.

Like all towns, there were some elitists. Mamaw and I were subject to this rude, elitist, snobbish behavior. There were some people who considered us inferior. There will always be experiences and people in our lives that hurt and disappoint. We know this, and we get over it. There is little to nothing any of us can do to change these misguided individuals. We are a better person for ignoring and discounting these people and the hurtful situations they create. This unkind and hurtful behavior should make us want to reach out to someone with kindness.

Rosiclare was often not good to me. I was considered the poor little grandchild with no parents. Some people referred to my situation as being orphaned. I was considered a child nobody wanted. But I had the love of my Mamaw, Pa, Aunt Lottie, Carole, and her mother and dad. These wonderful people enabled me to survive the hurt, shame, and stigma of being poor, orphaned, and ostracized by some people in Rosiclare. I just did not fit in their circle of the perfect family. Remember, in Rosiclare in the '50s and '60s, most all mothers and dads stayed together.

When I was growing up in Rosiclare, it was a dry town. It still is dry to this day. The residents who wanted beer, wine, and alcohol drove to Elizabethtown, which was three miles away. They still go there when thirsty. Elizabethtown back in the day was known for her drinking establishments. Sad to say, some people considered that worthy of being regarded as her claim to fame. Elizabethtown was the beer capital of Hardin County. Today nothing has changed. If you are so inclined to get thirsty, Elizabethtown can accommodate your desire for drink. I am sure some members of my dad's family who lived in Elizabethtown had a bar stool or two with their name on it. And I am also sure their bar stool was always occupied. Elizabethtown did not have many job opportunities. It was a small town comprised of people with most residents believing and living the core values found in good character and good individuality.

Rosiclare in the '50s and '60s had several churches. Everyone went to church. If you were not in church on Sunday morning, you were too sick to go anywhere or do anything.

Once a booming prosperous little mining town and home to Alcoa is now irretrievable. The only people who know and will remember Rosiclare are a few whose roots are still there. Main Street, the Fourth of July celebration on the Ohio River, snow ice cream, watching the great beauty of a sunrise and sunset over Rosiclare, and my good memories of Rosiclare's splendors of the past. Good memories last forever. I will always love Rosiclare. It was where I must have belonged from birth until high school graduation.

Growing up in small-town Rosiclare with three old people who loved me, wanted me, and never thought once about abandoning me has been one of my greatest strengths. My hometown; those three old people who raised me; my best friend, Carole; her parents, who helped guide me—all instilled in me the knowledge to protect what in life is important. I also love Rosiclare because it was home to Mamaw, Pa, and Aunt Lottie all their life. They say "home is where the heart is." Even though I have not lived in Rosiclare for the past fifty-seven years, and I will never go back there to live, Rosiclare will always have my heart. Rosiclare will always be my hometown. That is where it all began. A little four-room frame house, behind the grade school, and in front of the railroad tracks. I can still smell the stacks of smoke coming from the train.

Even though some experiences in my hometown made me feel less important than most people, I still love Rosiclare. We all have those kinds of experiences in our life; some more than others. I guess the only way to explain this behavior is to admit we are all humans. Human nature is not always kind. But because of where we started and where we are today and where we are going with our future, we will always remember everyone deserves kindness. We know the pain caused by those who think they are better than us, who lack smiles and a kind word. We will be aware and conscious of others' feelings. Kindness to someone is never forgotten, and we may never know how being kind to someone gave them hope and purpose.

> For he looked for a city which hath foundations, whose builder and maker is God. (Hebrews 11:10 KJV)

Our pain, caused by the abandonment of our parents, allows us to understand. We can share with all the emotional trauma donated to us by Mother and Dad. NEVER QUIT—NEVER GIVE UP.

My Home town Rosiclare

7

My Hero, My Mamaw

For those who say we live in a world where there are no longer heroes are mistaken, they just do not know where to look. My Mamaw, Carmel, was a hero! She lived her entire life in the very small town of Rosiclare, Illinois.

When my mother took off and left me with Mamaw, she failed to ask Grandmother if she could care for me. Mother failed to ask Mamaw if she wanted me. Mother did not care what the answer would have been. Her mind was decided. She did not want this baby girl and was determined to give this child away and out of her life.

In reality, there was no other family member to abandon me to. Every member of Dad's family cared nothing for my existence, as did Mother's family except for Mamaw and two other old people who have already been introduced to you. My precious Mamaw did want me. She considered this innocent, needy, helpless baby girl a blessing.

Our lives are decided, and they are determined by the choices we make. We make our choices and then those choices make us; protecting, nurturing, raising, and loving me—this infant grandchild—was the choice Mamaw made for the next eighteen years of her life.

29

This was her most rewarding, satisfying, welcoming, and heartwarming choice. It was a choice she never regretted. Instead, she loved the choice and decision she made.

Mamaw released the choice of raising me over to God in faith and prayer, asking for his strength and guidance in this enormous task finishing according to his will and his purpose. This choice made of Mamaw's own free will was God's absolute show of love and perfection. She was not afraid of the hardships and difficulties of raising me. She was strong, comfortable, and sure in her salvation and her relationship with Jesus Christ. She knew he would be present at all times in this choice, and she was right.

Mamaw's heart was unwavering when confronted with struggles and difficulties. She was always determined to give me a chance at a good life.

All fairy tales involve a rescue, and a rescue involves risk. Mamaw is like the heroine in a fairy tale. She put the next eighteen years of her life on hold intentionally, delaying anything and everything she might have desired so she could raise me. Mamaw was widowed and poor. She rarely bought herself anything. While Mother and Dad are living the life of friends, party, and laughter, Mamaw's days were spent working tirelessly to provide for their child. Mamaw could be defined by her actions and attitude, and not by her circumstances. Mamaw was a woman ahead of her time. She was her only voice.

She was a woman with a strong constitution and a clear vision. A woman of steadfast determination and constant intention. She was a decisive woman showing commitment to her goal managing the many challenges testing her. Mamaw was tenacious, strong-willed, never relinquishing her journey of achievement. Failure did not exist in her world. Failure was for quitters and slackers. Success belongs to the resolute and to the unshakables. The great weakness for most people is giving up. Success is obtained with hard work, tenacity, and mental strength to carry on. Success does not happen overnight.

Most of the time success takes a lot of patience and continuous struggle. Sometimes it takes years to achieve your goal. When success comes to you, you have shown courage and determination. Always take advantage of opportunity. Mamaw said, "Only winners never quit—only winners never give up."

Mamaw was poor by most everyone's definition. She was widowed before I was two years old. She raised me from infancy until I left home after high school graduation at the age of almost eighteen.

She made the choice and decision to take me at a time in her life that was already difficult. Her life was about to become even more difficult with great hardship. She would receive nothing from my mother and dad. To provide for me, the next eighteen years would be marked with backbreaking work. The years ahead of her, her future days would be filled with fatigue, exhaustion, and toilsome, endless grinding monotonous tasks of labor awarding very minimal income. Also a great heartache was on its way to Mamaw. My grandfather's health was failing, and this rested heavily on her mind with great sadness and concern. Grandfather did pass away. Now the very difficult and burdensome job I had placed in my grandparents' life was now on the shoulders of my Mamaw. She was alone.

Mamaw decided we would now make our home with Pa and Aunt Lottie. Mamaw supported me by washing and ironing for people, babysitting, and any other odd job she could find.

Rosiclare, like most small towns in the '50s and '60s, offered no jobs for women. Women stayed home and cared for their children and husband. Grandmother cooked, cleaned house, and did the laundry while at Pa's house. This also helped her dad, Pa, with her sister, Great-Aunt Lottie. Aunt Lottie was slightly mentally challenged. All this assistance Mamaw gave helped pay for our living with Pa and Aunt Lottie. The neglect of me by my mother and dad had become a burden once again for someone else. Great-Grandfather, Pa, and

Great-Aunt Lottie loved having us live with them. We were family and we loved and took care of one another.

Even though Mamaw and I loved Rosiclare, we were looked down on by some of the town's people. We were sometimes treated less important than others. We were often ignored and avoided as unworthy of notice or recognition. Mamaw was a widow raising a forgotten grandchild. She was financially broke. But unlike so many people of today, she never asked for or received anything from the government; everything she had was earned with diligent hard work. She stayed faithful to God's plan.

She was not afraid of hard work. She believed welfare robbed individuals of their dignity. She thought the only things Americans were entitled to was freedom, protection both domestic and foreign, and a good economy to support themselves and their family. She believed not asking people to work if they were able in return for government assistance was an insult. It robbed them of their respect and discipline. She considered it abuse and was offended when the government took hardworking taxpayers' money to support someone who can work but will not. And she expected her family to be like her, fiercely independent. Mamaw all her life shone as bright as the blazing hot Illinois sun. You knew where she stood on particular situations, positions, responsibilities, beliefs, and core values.

Mamaw was the illustration, the original design, the dawning of love, sacrifice, courage, ability, respect, honor, and promise. There are still people like that today. However, it seems we must look a little harder to find them.

In the winter, she would have people's clothes strung up all over the living room to dry. We had a big pot-bellied coal stove. In those days, there were no automatic washers and dryers. If there had been, Mamaw would not have had the money to purchase.

Mamaw had four laundries a week at $5 each. She had to pull the washer in off the porch and fill with water using the kitchen sink faucet and water hose. When finished with wash, she drained water and pulled washer back onto porch until tomorrow and another laundry. In the summer, she would hang clothes to dry outside. Illinois winters are cold and the summers are hot. She stood on her tired feet and legs washing and ironing those four laundries each week, making a total of $20. All this was done to support me. I got it all! The money she made was spent for my clothes, school supplies, doctor, dentist, and so on. Pa gave me a place to live, food, and utilities. Mamaw gave me the remainder of life's necessities and daily needs. Mamaw rarely was able to purchase anything for herself. For eighteen years, she dedicated her life to me, giving all her time, her energy, and her money to me. She always disregarded her wants and needs. She was never envious of what others were able to have and enjoy. The difficulties and challenges in her life were many. All were caused by the task of caring for me. The verbal abuse Mamaw had to endure when Mother came to our house for a visit was extreme. Mother intimidated, manipulated, humiliated, ridiculed, bullied, and intentionally hurt Mamaw. This cruel, calculated, repetitive pain happened almost every visit. Mamaw accepted this behavior out of concern. She was afraid if she put up a defense, Mother would take me to live with her. My dad was 100 percent absent from my life. He offered 100 percent of nothing to my upbringing. My dad's total contempt for me, his little girl, his willful hurtful display of resentment for my being born, handed me problems that still today occupy my heart, mind, and spirit. Again, because of me and my parents' abusive neglect and incivility, Mamaw was hurt.

Mamaw never complained, never expressed displeasure or lamented about having to raise me. Both my parents are worthy of being criticized as having reprehensible, obnoxious behavior when regarding their treatment of me. Mother's toxic personality and character caused much hurt and displeasure when in her presence. Neither parent helped with my care. Their dereliction of duty to me was shameful. They had given Grandmother a job most people would refuse.

Mamaw derived immense joy, happiness, and pleasure providing me with a nurturing and structured home environment in which to know I was loved and wanted.

Mamaw always searched for solutions to problems and never for an excuse. She believed her biggest advocate was the Holy Spirit. Her faith was strong. Her faith had no limits. It would have been easy for her to give up on this hard life. A lot of people would have understood her decision had she made that choice. Mamaw accepted the struggles and adversities handed her by Mother and Dad. She focused on things in her control. She knew she had been given a great purpose. She knew of her courage. She would never grow weak and give in to a victim defeated mentality.

Mamaw's dream and her purpose in life was to give me hope and a belief in a good future. Being mentally and physically exhausted, being financially lacking, she did not quit. The task of raising me alone with zero assistance of any kind from my parents was an emotionally, financially, and physically arduous job. She never thought of giving up. She viewed her life as being blessed. This attitude secured her strength and courage to carry on. The hardships in her life were only battles. She knew in the end she would win the war.

I had all the things I needed. I went to the doctor when I was sick. I visited the dentist two times a year, and I wore eyeglasses.

I had other things that were not essential requirements of life. However, they were basic as they related to a child feeling equal and not inferior to other children.

I always had a new Easter dress and shoes. Mamaw made sure I had a good Christmas, good birthday, and so on. All this was bought with $20 a week she would earn from backbreaking drudgery work—

the kind of work most people today would not consider doing. Not only would they not consider, they would never do that type of work. I was always a low-maintenance child, never asking for much of anything. I am still that way today. Even though Mamaw, Pa, and Aunt Lottie showered me with love and affection, there would always be that insecurity in just about every area of my life. This was a result of being abandoned by the two people who were supposed to love me the most. Their contempt for me was on display my entire life growing up in Rosiclare. We remember, but we should not dwell on the failures of our parents. We will not allow their lack of human decency to destroy us. We know our value is not determined by our parents' derelict disregard for us. Maybe we can share our story and help someone suffering as we do. We have survived the trauma of our parents considering us to be virtually unknown. Through our words, behavior, and actions, we can be an inspiration to others. We will show empathy toward them. We will not overprotect them. We will let them know we appreciate and validate who they are as an individual. This should increase their confidence and independence. We will encourage them to know they are equal to anyone. All people have experienced trauma and pain in their life. But the ones who go forward with a purposeful life are those who have done the work to clean up their wounds.

Our experience of being abandoned by our parents and all the negativities and pain that accompany this unfortunate situation can be utilized. We can use our very real acquaintance with parental neglect to help facilitate positive change for others' lives.

Mamaw was a woman of optimism. In reality, with all her struggles, most people would have found it impossible to be optimistic. Her actions were bold, persistent, and courageous. She was an inspiring woman teaching me to feel I was in charge of my life. She was teaching me self-confidence, self-determination, and responsibility. This was probably one of her biggest challenges. I was so lost in feeling discarded and left behind starting at a very early age and continuing long into my adult years. Because Mamaw did not quit and did not give up on herself and me, I went on to have a beautiful, fulfilling life, lacking in nothing. It took a long time for all her teachings, instructions, and coaching to resonate with me; however, they were all there the entire time.

I believe Mamaw was given the innate ability to never quit. It could not be found in her character to give up. How many times she would say, "Actions speak louder than words," "What someone does has more quality, importance, virtue, value, and merit than speaking their words," "Actions speak the truth," and "It takes no effort to lie with a chattering tongue."

Mamaw detested lying. She was an astute observer of people. This life's lesson, shared many times by her, has much truth and wisdom. Regrettably, we will witness this truth many times. Actions will always have an advantage over words.

I was always coached to never quit. Mamaw thought success without adversity, tribulation, and misfortune was empty and most always unachievable. She believed the harder you worked for something, the more you loved, appreciated, and protected it. She felt the sweet taste of success was far better when you earned your success. She knew a good life was rarely found in always looking for and traveling the easy road. She loathed the expression "if only." She thought these people lacking in initiative, taking no action, making excuses while waiting for their door of opportunity to open would prove to be disappointing. She felt they would never know their life to have purpose.

Mamaw knew love was not always pleasant and kind. It has a strict and harsh personality. I thought this show of her love to be nauseating. However, her undeviating faithfulness to obedience was love. She sacrificed all for me, and I was not her responsibility. Her actions showed me a person's life is never meant to be all about themselves, but rather about the persons around them. Following through on this action will give results in pleasure for all involved. Mamaw was convinced happiness and contentment were in hard work, integrity, and character. She taught arrogance, selfishness, materialism, and jealousy brought sadness and worry to our lives. Taking the easy way out of life's encounters, be it personal or job related, leads to disappointment and, most often, regret. Taking the easy way will invariably contribute to failure, aggravation, and underachievement. Look around, and you will see this lazy and timid character is a waste. This character cannot be trusted or taken seriously. Stay committed and disciplined to your core values.

Mamaw was fair with discipline. She was loving but firm. You understood she was in control. Mamaw had no problem expressing her point of view and her reasoning for not backing down on what she felt should be my discipline. She knew my life would be a reflection of her teaching. She always gave 100 percent. Unfortunately, I have made mistakes. But without the memory of her teaching, I would have made many more.

Mamaw also wanted a good life for mother. Mother always had a mind of her own, even as a young girl. She did not learn from her mistakes. She was always a person out of control. I do not believe mother wanted to cause confrontation. Her words and actions led you to believe the root of her hostility was narcissistic. My mother would say to me many times with a loud and raised expression, "If something happens to you, what happens to me when I get old?" She never cared for anyone but herself. She was always unable to control her fits of anger. She must have all the attention. We all have undesirable errors and defects in our personality and character. We do not always desire these defects, but they are there. None of us are perfect. Mother displayed her harmful and damaging barrage of words to everyone she knew sooner or later in their relationship. Her words and violent anger would break suddenly without warning. It was anyone's guess what would cause her words to erupt like a brutal volcano. No one in her path was spared, especially Mamaw. I was raised by 3 elderly family members: Mamaw, Pa, and Aunt Lottie, who were agreeable almost to a fault. They were a quiet bunch. All my life

I never heard Mamaw tell a lie, say an ugly, angry, offensive word, or speak badly of anyone. She could always defend herself and win with the truth. She was direct, brief, and to the point. She could seem abrupt if necessary but always gave respect to the participant. She was engaging in conversation. She did not argue. Always declared if you argue, you lose the conversation and eliminate everything that could add value to your discussion. She stood up for her beliefs and principles and thought right would prevail. She believed a person's word was one of the most valuable, noble, qualities, and possessions an individual can own. If your word means nothing, you have nothing.

She lived and indoctrinated to work hard, save her money, be disciplined, speak the truth, keep her word, live and play by the rules, be loyal, be accountable for herself, have consistency and stability, be of service, make everyone feel needed and important, create a climate that is positive, take advantage of opportunity, stand for right regardless of who is committing the wrong, never waver on her beliefs and values, invest her money and invest in her eternity, and always acknowledge that the eternity investment guaranteed a larger and longer-lasting reward. Every day my Mamaw spent time alone with God in prayer. My Mamaw never owned stock, never had a 401-K, CD, IRA, and probably never had a saving account in a bank. But she knew how to save and manage what little money she did own. That $20 a week went a long way in providing for me. For me, this little grandchild, my Mamaw was one of the richest ladies on this earth. After all, she provided me with every financial necessity while growing up. She could be defined for the sacrifices she made to ensure my life would be happy and blessed. To me, Mamaw meant love, hope, and promise.

Doing without and hard work did not drain her energy and passion from her goal of my future. They restored her, revitalized her, and made her resolute. To her, exhaustion meant she was conquering her goal for me. She was honoring God's plan for her life. It was a hard life, a difficult plan to follow, but she stayed faithful.

Mamaw was not like most people. She was stronger than most people, stronger in courage, determination, stamina, and faith. I always believed her inherent strong will was a big contributor. Her will was an inseparable quality. Her mental, physical, and spiritual strengths would surpass all expectations.

Mamaw did not feel pity for excuses and apology makers. She considered them to be a cop-out and guise. She perceived wishy-washy decision-making people as having no backbone, and she detected they could not be trusted or believed.

My Mamaw's legacy is selfless devotion, always with a vision to advance greatness. Her life was bold and unafraid. She experienced miracles in her life because faith and prayer produce them every day. Raising me was one of her miracles. She believed in the future she could not yet see for me. And her reward would be to one day see my future she believed in and made happen. She saw the future for me she dreamed, prayed for, and directed before she passed away.

It is not what we have in our life but who we have in our life that matters. It is what you do and make happen for others and not what you gain for yourself that lasts and will be remembered for generations. I hope you have someone in your life such as my Mamaw. I was an abandoned infant, and people react differently to situations. However, my inner self, my own individual internal identity was weakened and broken so critically and dangerously by my parents. It would have been necessary for me to have a person such as Mamaw to help me overcome the injury my parents caused. It was still many years into adulthood until I was able to cope and feel somewhat equal and worthy. Obviously, I was given a weak nature that would require a lot of work. I hope your core, your inmost soul, is stronger than mine was. I hope you nurture your every hope and dream. We do not have to let the neglect of our parents control and ruin our life. We got off to a bad start, but we can make our finish good. Believe in yourself and NEVER QUIT—NEVER GIVE UP!

When thou passest through the waters, I will be with thee; and through the rivers, they shall not overflow thee; when thou walkest through the fire, thou shall not be burned; neither shall the flame kindle upon thee. (Isaiah 43:2 KJV)

Mamaw was a woman of discipline, certainty, and substance. She was one of the most humble individuals I have ever known. She always displayed an absence of pride, arrogance, jealousy, and pretense. She silently blessed me with all the good, free gifts life has to offer. She was a rock. Her wisdom, her always living in reality, her down-to-earth nature, and her practical teaching gave me a desire for a good life. Mamaw was always alert, clever, all-knowing, and savvy. She was a hands-on, loving, influential role model for service and good. She was armed with very little money but had an abundance of common sense. Common sense and prudent judgment are important qualities. Without them, your life will be lived on the edge of a slippery slope headed downhill, causing harm and unfortunate circumstances to you and, possibly, others.

She said to think positively, to expect something and work hard to make it happen. She told me to invest a large heart and mind in my dreams. She taught that if my dreams had a kinship to reality, they could be achieved, and they would come true. She was right. Passionate people are unstoppable. Their enthusiasm drives them toward accomplishment. Mamaw said, "People who never have a dream never have a dream come true." Those simple and few choice words will start motivation and get results.

Mamaw lectured that honesty was the foundation for everyone to have a less complicated and more rejoicing life. She taught that hard work fueled and heightened success. Being prudent was being wise. Loyalty was crucial in triumphant relationships, careers, and job performance. Passion, devotion, and obligation to duty on the job would create opportunity and respect. Mamaw had the unique traits of being tenacious, insistent, and tough. Mamaw had no other choice but to be tough. I was a heavy and towering responsibility for her. After all, she was a grandmother and not getting any younger. And with Grandfather's passing, she was alone. Her only daughter, my mother, was disobedient and disrespectful. What if I too had those delinquent, disruptive, rebellious behavioral similarities? But invariably, she had confidence in her decision to care for me from six months of age until eighteen years old. I did not have a lot, but I had all I needed. I had an abundance of love. I never had to worry about Mamaw abandoning me for any reason.

You have heard the expression, "An army of sheep led by a lion will defeat an army of lions led by a sheep." It is true. Everything starts at the head and goes down. Everyone follows their leader—a strong pastor, a strong church, a strong woman, a strong man, a strong family, a strong business owner, a strong business, a strong president, a strong America, and so on. I always saw my Mamaw as the lion leading the sheep, her family, and friends. She had many nieces and nephews. They all admired her for her wisdom. She never complained. She possessed a servant's spirit. She offered them advice, praise, and encouragement. She was assertive but respectful. Mamaw was an advocate of anyone needing help and aid. She gave strength, energy, and invigorated others to stand on truth, principle, and honor. She was a leader. She was plain-spoken, direct, a true communicator with no flattery. She did not waste time with her talk. She took prudent risks when aiming for the big prize, her goal, and her dream. She most definitely would stand up and defend herself. She would state her case with certainty, conviction, and clarity, just as she did at her beloved church. And if the situation was bad enough, she would only pass and repass with individuals involved. She said to forgive but do not forget. In other words, she was not going to hold out her hand and let the same people bite her again. She would speak when she saw you, help you if you needed help. However, she would not intentionally be found in your company. It took a lot to anger Mamaw. Remember, we walked to the church for years in all kinds of weather while being passed by her church members. Pass and repass meant you were present in her heart, but she would not be available

41

to witness, accept, tolerate, or suffer your bad behavior. A person cannot be honest themselves if they are afraid to offend someone for being ill-behaved.

She treated people the way she wanted to be treated. She told me to never bully anyone but not to run from a bully.

I was trained to stand up for myself, clarify my position, have compassion for myself, and set boundaries for myself with the people who are mistreating me. Always speak truth to power; an expression of courage to call attention to anyone when oppression has reared its ugly head. And doing it with no regrets no matter who they are or what position or status they dominate. Do this without fiery expressions or insults, without temper and anger, no profanity and long sermons. This only makes bad consequences for all and solves nothing. Stay calm, do not retaliate, and speak only for yourself. Be respectful always. But most of all, state your case and walk away. All this will assure your win and give your aggressor something to think about.

She directed me to accept approval when I did right and accept guilt when I did wrong. She coached to listen to your conscience, which gives to all the ability to distinguish between right and wrong. This will remind you of the principles, values, and rules that will make the people you love proud. Life is hard for everyone. However, the explanation and instruction Mamaw imparted will create many more happy days than days of trouble and sadness. All this teaching resonated with me growing up, but I did not put a lot of it to use until my adult years.

Mamaw did not give in, give up, or give way in trials of commanding emotions or influence. She faced with audacity, assurance, bravery, boldness, and fortitude the many hurdles and obstacles in her life with perseverance. She never shared a problem or concern with me. And there had to be many. Raising a baby aged six months to late teenage years without Grandfather at a time when there were few jobs available to women. There were no jobs available to women in Rosiclare to a widow raising an infant grandchild. She had to always be concerned and worried about Mother—concerned about the decisions she was making for her life. Mamaw never gave me a reason to think I was not wanted, not loved, or that I was a burden. She always strived to make certain I felt secure, protected, wanted, and loved. All this in Rosiclare at a time in life when prejudice and bias were rampant. Mamaw's suffering produced perseverance and character. Her quality of never quitting, never giving up, was the commander in her life. Many times she would smile when a tear felt more suitable for the situation. She was always prepared to stay the course. Even as she was hardest hit with difficulty she would continue slowly along. She instilled if circumstances seem hopeless, you must not quit, you must not give up. You cannot succeed at anything if you own a defeatist attitude.

The most valuable gifts I received from Mamaw were free. They would be called human decency with all the good attributes it will retain in your character. The exposing of human decency will affect every occasion, every detail, and every individual in your life.

Mamaw and I spent a lot of time together. Spending time together was about all Rosiclare had to offer any resident. We had no money and no vehicle; therefore, much quality time was available. Mamaw used a great deal of this time to mentor me with her wise counseling.

There was a glider on my front porch as far back in my childhood as I can remember. Mamaw had many talks in that porch glider. Her conversations were always genuine. Her talk was never wasted. I was being taught many of life's valuable lessons. I was taught to always be grateful for all I had been given. That difficulty, disappointments, and misfortune visits everyone. I was told life offers no escape for these tagalongs. They are never invited, but they manage to show up anyway. I was instructed to show my intruder they were never part of my life's plan. The lessons in that front porch glider taught me that when these tagalongs came, it was okay to be discouraged. But it was never okay to quit. She said my response to these nuisances would be to work even harder. She told me to take siege and attack them with the will to achieve and overcome. Mamaw did the job every day of caring for me with never an utter of annoyance or bitterness. She embarked on this enormous job every day for eighteen long years wearing a smile. She did this being happy and content while Mother and Dad were putting all their emotion, action, and all their existence to making sure they were not burdened with their child—the child they both unwelcomed, abandoned, and refused. Mamaw worked in the front porch glider. She spent hours every summer getting vegetables from Pa's big garden ready for canning. She would be peeling, shucking, washing, snapping, and shelling. We always had plenty to eat because of Pa's garden and Mamaw's canning. Her pantry was complete with a large variety of canned garden vegetables. She always managed to prepare enough to last our family with food until Pa's next harvest. Mamaw could cook a rich man's dinner with vegetables from the garden. Her seasoning was the best. Everything loaded in bacon grease, fatback, with even more butter and salt. Mamaw kept her family fed and happy.

Once every summer, Mamaw would somehow save enough money to buy a bushel of apples and peaches. She and I would sit in that old glider and peel. I knew this meant numerous apple pies and peach cobbler were in my future.

We would sit in that glider and watch the fireworks over the Ohio River on the Fourth of July. Rosiclare always had a big Fourth of July celebration. We could see the fireworks from my front porch. We read our library books together while making use of the old faithful glider on my front porch. Mamaw and Carole's mother would visit often in the porch glider. No doubt, their many conversations involved the two little girls they adored. Two godly women with all the right answers to mine and Carole's many questions. These women had the necessary medicine for all our cuts, scratches, bruises, and sometimes, wounded hearts. Mamaw and Hazel's medicine was hugs, kisses, and assurance. These women never grew weary of me and

Carole needing them and leaning on them to provide all our essential needs. Mamaw and Hazel's strength was a result of their relationship with God. I am sure my grandmother's and Hazel's prayers regarding me and Carole were addressed this way: beginning with "please" and ending with "thank you." That old porch glider proved to be as educational and resourceful as any classroom. The service that glider provided still exists today in the lives of me and Carole. I look back at my life in amazement at the examples of God's little things he uses to keep us in companionship with him. A front porch glider probably purchased at the secondhand store was among his many meaningful gifts—a front porch glider that helped to nurture, elevate, heighten, and intensify my love, respect, and admiration for Mamaw. Mamaw knew what she was accomplishing. She was using the porch glider to strengthen, maintain, preserve, and keep always in my heart the determination for a good life. Mamaw gave my opportunity.

We went blackberry picking every year. We would make blackberry cobbler and many jars of blackberry preserves. Mamaw was a wonderful cook. She could prepare a good and nutritious meal with only garden vegetables. Her seasoning was the best. The only day we had meat was Sunday—always the same: fatty gristle pork chops one Sunday and fried chicken the next Sunday. We never ate beef, not even ground beef. Great-Grandfather, Pa, did not like beef. I imagine this is why beef was never served.

I always had a birthday party with the same four or five neighborhood children. These were kids Carole and I would play with on occasion. Mamaw gave me two new bicycles. Both bicycles were given as birthday presents. My first bicycle was a twenty-inch. When I outgrew it, she bought another for a different birthday, a new twenty-six-inch bicycle. She purchased both bicycles at the Rosiclare Western Auto store on their layaway plan. The bicycles cost $20 back then. The $20 was a week's income for Mamaw. I will never know a person like my Mamaw who worked so hard did without for herself and sacrificed so much so that a grandchild could have things like other children. My mother and dad gave no thought to the distress they gladly gave me and Mamaw. My grandmother always made my favorite cake. We had ice cream for my birthday. She baked often, but ice cream was a rarity. We did not have the money to purchase confectionery food and drink. The only soft drinks I had growing up were at Carole's house.

I never, not one time, received a birthday call, card, or gift from dad. He was absent 100 percent of the time. Mother always brought me a gift on or close to my birthday. Mamaw always managed to save enough so I could have like other children. She never wanted me to feel different. Unfortunately, I did feel different. After all, back in the 1950s and 1960s, everyone in Rosiclare had parents. To my knowledge, during the time I was in Rosiclare schools, kindergarten through grade 12, I was the only child being raised by a grandmother. No one else lacked parents. There are a lot more children today being abandoned by parents than there were in the '50s and '60s. However, the trauma, the insecurity, and the feelings of being unworthy have not changed. The harm done to children who are abandoned as infants, by a mother, a dad, or both will never change. The difference is how the child deals with parents' neglect.

You know you are not alone. You know you did not cause them to leave you. And you promise yourself their disregard for you will not keep you from a happy and purposeful life. My parents gave me away at six months old, and they never looked back. It took until my adult years for me to begin to deal effectively and attempt to overcome difficulties. God was patient and waited for me to accept his plan for my life. God has a good plan for each and every life. But we have to accept his plan for us. I was loved and I was both blessed and privileged to be raised by my precious Mamaw. But being abandoned by both parents did affect me immensely. I went on to have a wonderful life of love, family, and success. Even after all these years and so many important people in my life, I am still troubled by being given away. But I refuse to allow my parents' decision to lie so heavy on my heart and mind that it weighs me down. I won't let them keep me from being happy.

Mamaw always made sure I had a good Christmas. We always had a tree. I never remember not having a white Christmas. It might not start snowing until Christmas Eve night but there would always be snow on the ground Christmas morning. Our house was filled with the pleasant tantalizing aroma of Christmas dinner. Mamaw canned everything from Pa's big garden. Therefore, we always had plenty to eat. Lots of canned vegetables, beans, and cornbread. But meat was lacking. The only time we had fruit, nuts, and candy was Christmas. Those items were not in our food budget. Knowing this, Carole's mother, Hazel, shared with me often. For Christmas, we always had a big healthy meal.

I always had a new Easter dress, shoes, and bonnet. Carole and I always had big Easter baskets. I can remember more than once walking to church Easter Sunday with snow covering my new white Easter shoes. Illinois weather in March and April can sometimes be harsh. It can be stormy, choppy, cold, and wet. It might even snow. The weather made me and Mamaw physically uncomfortable. However, it did not stop us walking to church. I always went to the beauty shop at Easter for a permanent.

I was a big kid and somehow I fell off the sliding board. My arm was hurt, and Mamaw rocked me all night. I whimpered all night with the hurt arm, and I was so big my feet touched the floor. Beyond any doubt, I was too big to be rocked. Mamaw knew I was hurting and she was always there for me.

We loved watching wrestling. Our television was twenty-one-inch black and white purchased at the used furniture store. I remember being with Mamaw when she bought it. Rosiclare had a public library. Mamaw and I would visit the library on Saturday afternoon to read and check out books. I believe Mamaw loved reading detective novels. Every time we went to town, we walked. It was a minimum of one and a half miles each way. Friday was grocery day. We would walk to the grocery store, and the store clerks would bring us home with the groceries.

I was a sophomore in high school, and Mamaw began dating her first boyfriend for a short time. He was widowed, and he wanted to marry Mamaw. Life for her would have been a lot easier. He would not let her bring me to live with them should they marry. Mamaw told him she would not leave me and she broke up with him. Mamaw loved me unconditionally. I always took priority over everything in her life. Mamaw always had time for me. She was always available with interest and kind words of encouragement suitable and worthy of the situation. She was a good listener and a good communicator.

Mamaw was a smart woman. She was on every occasion aware of what was happening. In other words, she did not wear rose-colored glasses. Growing up, I never grew hungry for hugs, kisses, and high-fives. We always had a good relationship. My personality was totally opposite of my mother's. It was always a pleasure for me to be in the company of my grandmother. I always felt I had been granted a special advantage, a favored benefit, a blessing available only to me. I will always love, respect, and show gratitude for Mamaw. No one knows what made mother so angry and difficult her entire life. I have often wondered if she might have been bipolar. She was always defiant and acting out with aggression, being spiteful and vindictive. Maybe if she had sought help, her life would have been different.

I am convinced the only time I caused Mamaw pain was when I left Rosiclare after high school graduation. I went to Jacksonville, Illinois. We both cried the day I left. She knew I must leave Rosiclare to have the kind of life she wanted, she prayed for, and sacrificed so much to give me. I had always been quiet, shy, passive, reserved, and withdrawn. I suppose I could be an introvert. I wage a constant battle with myself to become likable. I have always experienced loneliness and fear of socializing. Some of my personality traits changed as I grew older and became a wife, mother, and business owner. I accept the change to be positive. However, I am still a stranger to social acceptability. I am still met with dismiss, overlook, and apparent and calculating rejection by some.

I lived in Jacksonville until I married. I lived there from early June 1965 until January 26, 1969. Early in 1966, I purchased a new red Volkswagen Beetle. I went to Rosiclare every other weekend to visit Mamaw, Pa, and Aunt Lottie. They were the only family I had ever known. I came along in each of their lives when they needed a reason to continue with meaning, to share their love and warmth, and to fulfill a promise to God. God gave them a purpose they longed for; he gave them me! I was loved, spoiled, and pampered always. I never caused them trouble or took advantage of their affection and love for me.

Mamaw had enormous courage. She revealed courage every day, always making tough decisions aligning with her values and principles. She made those decisions with determination, grit, strong will, and fortitude. She had the strength and courage to follow through on actions that were right but difficult. Mamaw was bold and she was audacious. If the unpopular action was the correct action, she took it. You would never hear Mamaw apologize for standing with truth and right. She would always go after the difficult challenge like a champion.

My Mamaw heard a little granddaughter's cry for help, and she answered. I hope and I know she can see the miracle and the future she wanted and believed for my life. The life she guided, nurtured, influenced to give character and substance. A good life she dreamed and hoped for me. A life that would meet with her approval.

I believe my every goal, my every accomplishment, my every dream, she placed in my heart and mind. God has given me so many blessings. The first blessing I received was him placing me, at six months of age, in the arms of Mamaw. God was telling Mamaw her little granddaughter had no one; therefore, he was putting the grandchild in her care, custody, and control. He was saying to Grandmother he knew she would follow his plan for my life. He also assured her to not fear because he would never leave us. Like all God's promises, he stayed with us all the way to the end. And he is still with me today.

Mamaw's battle plan for my life was serious. It was clearly outlined, detailed, and defined in her mind. Her plan for me was incapable of failing. She began very early in my life applying ground rules, guidance, and protocol, which would assure her battle plan for me a victory. These rules were needed to accomplish her goal. They served as my reminder to trust in myself. She had authored the foundation for how I was expected to place value with direction and purpose in all aspects of my life. Never trembling in fear but charging ahead in courage and faith. I was always a good obedient soldier. The same ground rules I listened to and adhered to were basic principles that would determine my future. Mamaw took a grandchild to raise that was not her responsibility. She never regretted that decision. She sacrificed so much, worked so hard, and never received as much as a dime from mother and dad. They gave nothing to help provide for my well-being and my comfort. It took all the money Mamaw could make to support me. She rarely was able to buy herself anything.

You love yourself, respect yourself, live with compassion and generosity for those in need. Live by the core values, principles, and traditions that have made America the best, most free, and with the largest Christian population known to mankind. Believe in yourself. You are important. God has you in His grip, and He is not letting go. He has a plan for your life. Hold your head high!

My grandmother will always be my hero. I have been let down by most of my family. I have always been short on friends. I have been shunned and ignored by people my entire life. But I found love, happiness, purpose, and achievement, and I attained what was important to a good life. I applied and put into practice what my grandmother wanted for my life. My grandmother did not live long enough to see the complete realization of her dream for me. But she lived long enough to see the battle plan she had for my life was won. She was happy. She never quit. She never gave up!

I was a child no one wanted, no one loved, no one intended to be bothered with, no one considered to be of any value, and to my parents and most family members, I was missing and absent. I did not exist. I did not meet their requirements to belong to and have a rightful place in my own family. I was considered a misfortune. This unwanted baby girl was going to be someone's heavy burden. This reality caused mother and dad's family to be annoyed with me, expunging me from their memory, consciousness, and our family record book. But God knew I only needed one family member. He controlled the perfect solution and he placed me in Mamaw's heart and loving arms.

All the good that has ever or will ever come my way is credited to Mamaw. God placed what seemed like an impossible responsibility on the shoulders of my aging, financially broke, widowed grandmother. He would not force her to love me, he would not force her to take me to raise, and he would not force her to want me. But he knew her decision before he laid on her heart this huge and always challenging task. God knew her love, patience, and care for me would be as vast as the ocean. My Mamaw deserves and receives from me all the credit, respect, and admiration I can increasingly accumulate today and every day of my life.

I lost Mamaw in 1986. She was eighty years young. She was alert and on top of her game right up to the end. She is still guiding my footsteps and spearheading my way through life. She was the wisest, the most courageous, the most determined, and the most extraordinary woman I will ever come to know.

Mamaw's loud expression and her enthusiasm of advice for a happy, purposeful, successful life was to always try again. NEVER QUIT—NEVER GIVE UP. These days she is in constant request to God asking for his hand to never leave me. Just like when I was a child, he is honoring her request.

Mamaw is still assuring me that she will never abandon me. She is still showing me wisdom. Today I remember her strength and courage when life brings trouble. Today she knows of my hard work and is proud. Her life's example still gives me intrepidity to conquer my fears. Today she gives to me her armor so I may defend myself. Her humility put her life on hold so I could have a good life. Her voice of optimism always meant to focus on goals, dreams, and not obstacles, the past, or regrets. Today the remembrance of her love assures me I am equal to anyone. Today she tells me no matter how busy I am, I should keep my daily appointment with God. She has taught me to keep my biggest life's ambition on my eternal home. Today and always Mamaw is present in my day-to-day life. She is still today caring for the little abandoned grandchild whose life she saved.

Like every child, I will not always heed her teaching. Therefore, today she reminds me of her sense of right I observed as a child. And she suggests to me I do not disappoint her.

Today grandmother knows she survives forever in the hearts and lives of mine and Gary's two daughters. Today she knows her legacy reaches as far as my grandchildren. Today I know God is saying to my grandmother, "You followed my plan, of which I am proud." Today my Mamaw knows I will NEVER QUIT—NEVER GIVE UP. Today I am living "what God will do!"

> I have fought a good fight, I have finished my course, I have kept the faith. (II Timothy 4:7 KJV)

Raising me, Mamaw faced many hardships out of her control. She faced them all with courage, undeniable, unyielding determination. Mamaw was relentless. She was strong when others were not. She had no husband, no money, not a lot of education, and no support from my parents, and she held no position of status in her hometown. The only things that gave her strength, made her relentless to survive, to achieve, were her never-give-up attitude and her faith. Her aspirations for my future kept her motivated and allowed her to keep finding her hidden strength.

She defeated every challenge testing her ability, every unwelcome circumstance, every opposing conflict, every resentment and nonacceptance, every doubt, every heartbreak, every sadness, every emotional, physical, and financial misfortune—all done because she loved this grandchild. Her heart was decided, and she had no regrets. Her faith was strong, giving her the power to continue forward through difficult, complicated, unpleasant occurrences and predicaments. She prayed to God many times about this forgotten grandchild, and she knew he was listening. She would never grow weary because she was doing her best, she was doing good for the grandchild she loved, and she was honoring God.

I showed and told Mamaw many times in life how much I loved her. I will be able to tell her again someday that she gave my life a chance when all others wanted nothing to do with me. Mamaw prevailed over many hardships and struggles with an impressive victory. This victory, I am sure, was surprising, mind-boggling, and eye-popping to the naysayers of my family and the residents of Rosiclare. Many family members did not want her to take me to raise. Mamaw always told me to be brave. She told me I was never alone. She knew God's miracles would be mine and her reward. She knew God keeps his promise!

Mamaw never regretted, never grieved, never cried, never felt sorry or pitied, never felt blame because she was given the job of raising me. She loved me, wanted me, and considered me a gift from God. She is the closest person to an angel I will ever know.

Raising me from infancy to adulthood was my Mamaw's calvary. She was widowed and alone. She was poor. Many times, her heart was broken. Her life held many broken days. Her aging body was often tired and broken. Her finances were always broken. But Mamaw's courage, spirit, and faith were never broken. Her love and devotion to me was never broken. God had given to my Mamaw a directive. She was to love and nurture this little forsaken grandchild. He commanded her to ensure this grandchild an opportunity for a good life. The command God gave Mamaw was never broken. And God's faithfulness to me and Mamaw is everlasting and never broken.

Me and MaMaw

MaMaw

Me and MaMaw, my Wedding

8

My Mamaw's Great Disappointment, Her Church

I am going to share a true and memorable story with you about my Mamaw leaving her church. This was the only church she had ever been a member of. It was very painful for my Mamaw, and she grieved over leaving. I know that the disrespect and deliberate, obvious arrogant actions shown to my grandmother and me by some church members wounded her heart. Their behavior toward us was inconsiderate, unnecessary, and unconscionable. Some members' behavior and attitude toward us were out of the realm of Christian conduct.

Mamaw never backed down, and she always did what she believed to be right. She was always respectful, straightforward, and unemotional. She never embellished the facts; truth could have been her name.

Mamaw could no longer tolerate the apathetic and callous disregard of some church members toward her and her little granddaughter. These actions had occurred for years. It took her a long time, but now she was putting an end to this difficult chapter in our lives.

To this day, I still love that little church in Rosiclare. I know Mamaw does too. This church is where, as a very young child, I was taught about Jesus. I attended this church as far back in my youth as I can remember. I stopped going somewhere around twelve years old.

Mamaw always believed that God wanted you to defend yourself but always to do so with respect and truth. She always said to be kind when putting forth your defense.

Mamaw was given this cross to bear. Her church had, for a very long time, refused to even acknowledge her attendance. She had been coping and praying about an answer to this situation. However, what I am about to tell you happened was deplorable, flagrant, and could no longer be condoned. She had been tolerating this treatment for years. But the result of this particular situation was cruel and mean to me and my grandmother. It proved to be humiliating to the church members, bringing attention to their shameful actions.

This time, for the first and only time, Mamaw called out their reprehensible behavior. She felt obligated to make known to some members their hypocrisy. I was present that Wednesday evening. I witnessed her testimony. I was proud of the way she had handled the situation. I will never forget that evening. Mamaw was a woman of courage. She always said to be truthful in all you say and to show integrity in all you do.

My Mamaw and Papaw attended and helped support this church financially. They helped to grow it in membership and spiritually, and they were some of its first members. They raised my mother and Uncle Ben in this church. And now Mamaw had me in this church every time the doors opened.

Several of the church members made Mamaw feel unwanted, not needed, and unwelcome. They made her feel inferior and insignificant. When Papaw was alive and this was their church, all was good. But now she was poor, widowed, and with an abandoned grandchild to raise all by herself. The church members changed because she no longer fit their definition of a suitable and accepted family.

She knew she had to move to another church. This burden had become too worrisome and troubling. Given the rude, haughty, and proud behavior of the church members, she was forced to make her decision.

Before I tell you this story, I ask that you read the following Bible scripture:

> Let your speech be always with grace, seasoned with salt, that ye may know how ye ought to answer every man. (Colossians 4:6 KJV)

As I stated before, this little church is where I received all my early childhood biblical teachings and instructions. This small church provided me, at a very young age, a strong foundation of Christianity to follow, making a life that Mamaw, Pa, and Aunt Lottie could be proud of.

We are being told in the above scripture to add worth and merit to our conversation. A Christian's talk should be helpful and of value. But we are to add the salt to the conversation so it will be seasoned and preserved. This will keep it alive, prevent it from being forgotten in the minds of the guilty. We are to be pleasant but firm. We are to defend ourselves against people who harm us emotionally or in any other way. As Christians, we are to present the truth using genuine words, showing Christ lives in us, always with the content of our conversation being understood. Putting a little salt in your message keeps the message alive and keeps it working in their minds, hearts, and souls. The salt flavors the good conscience we all have and do not exercise enough. The salt will be their soap, their cleanser.

At last, this is why Mamaw finally decided to say goodbye to her church. After Papaw passed away in May 1949, Mamaw stayed faithful to their church. She and I walked to every service. The only time we missed church was when we were sick. We had no vehicle, and the walk was approximately two and a half miles one way. We walked to church, and we walked home from church every Sunday morning, every Sunday evening, and to prayer meeting every Wednesday evening. We walked in the rain, the snow, the cold, and in the hot summer heat. The church was small, probably somewhere between forty and fifty people in attendance each service. We walked everywhere we went; we had no vehicle. We were the only ones walking. We knew everyone, and everyone knew us. Mamaw walked all those times after working so hard doing people's laundry so she could support me.

I still remember vividly that Wednesday night service and my Mamaw's testimony. Mamaw and I were walking to church like we always did. There came suddenly a very heavy and violent pouring rainstorm. We witnessed four vehicles with church members going to our church. They all passed us like they always did, never stopping to ask if we would like to ride. To this day, I remember who they were. They all were neighbors and lived close by. They all lived within a mile from our house. We all lived in a neighborhood community in Rosiclare called Fairview. Fairview was comprised of Alcoa-owned homes occupied by Alcoa employees and their families.

We arrived at church soaked—I mean really soaked, dripping wet from the violent rainstorm. Now, we had walked many times before in bad weather but never anything that came close to this. After the service, if a member wanted, the minister offered them the opportunity to give their testimony.

Mamaw and I were at the back of the church, sitting on the last pew. When Mamaw spoke, she was very respectful. She reminded them how she and Papaw were members and supported the church, raised their family in the church, and now she was raising her little granddaughter in that church.

She told them that evening how they passed us, allowing us to be soaked in the rain. She told them that evening she would never attend church there again. Mamaw was kind and respectful, but she was factual. She made them realize how insensitive they had been. She told them they had no concern for others and she questioned their honor, integrity, and decency. She left nothing on her heart that night; she spilled it all. She told them they did not respect her and her granddaughter; therefore, she needed to set relational boundaries with them. Her testimony was so powerful and so resonating that many church members that evening followed us home after church, offering us a ride. Of course, she refused them and would not get in their car. She refused them because she knew she had put them on display and she knew their heart was not in helping me and her.

Mamaw's testimony was delivered by and gifted with the Holy Spirit. God guided her that evening to say the right things in the polite and most gracious manner, overflowing with the truth. We had been walking to every service we attended at that church since Papaw passed away ten years earlier, and the same four couples/members passed us every time and never stopped to ask us to ride with them.

Mamaw always kept her word. She never attended service at that little church that had meant so much to both of us. We did attend faithfully another church in Rosiclare. Mamaw never moved her membership. One of her friends and neighbors took us to church and brought us home. This was a blessing because this church was further away, and the walk would have been much longer. I think Mamaw felt like the church she had been a member of and supported most of her adult life did not care. After all, they did not receive much more than $2 a week, which was 10 percent of her weekly income. She would never force herself on anyone or go where she was not wanted. She was the kind of woman who was good to everyone, always trying to do what was right and what would honor God. She expected the same of others, especially the people she worshipped with in church. I think she honored God that Wednesday evening.

She was bringing attention to the disrespect she had been receiving for a long time. She made known the truth of the unholy behavior of her fellow Christians. She spoke the truth with kindness and humility. She flavored the truth with salt.

Mamaw's integrity would call you out for wrongdoing. She called them out for their unrighteous behavior.

Mamaw and I walked to that church for years, and not one time were we asked to ride with people living in very close proximity to our house. They were going to the same church. Mamaw's decision to leave her church was warranted. She had been hurt, and she had been made to feel inferior and unimportant. The Christian bond in her church had been broken. We were the only members attending church who had to walk to the services.

My best friend Carole and her mother attended the same church as me and Mamaw. Carole and her mother rode to church service with one of the neighbors. It was not their fault they were offered a ride to church, and we were not. Carole's mother, Hazel, did not drive. I do not know what happened, but shortly after Mamaw stopped attending the church, Carole and Hazel did too. I do know if Hazel could drive, she most assuredly would have driven me and Mamaw to and from church service. Carole and I are still going to church; however, we are going to separate churches in Rosiclare.

Several years ago, on a visit to Rosiclare, I attended Sunday morning service at the church of my youth. I sat in the same pew, in the same place my Mamaw sat the Wednesday evening she gave her decisive testimony. The evening she told of her decision to leave her church, a church that housed so many memories of her and my Papaw worshipping there, enjoying the fellowship with believers, helping to build the church membership, and being in God's word, the Bible.

My Mamaw's calm, respectful, and truthful testimony revealed the hurt she was feeling. It revealed the unhappiness caused by members' lack of knowing or caring about their wrong behavior. She wondered if they even had the decency or ability to think of others. Their actions for many years were more than just a show of bad manners. Her testimony was kind, but it did suggest bold disregard for the standards of Christian character on display in that church. I was old enough to think the church members treated us this way because they felt superior to us. They all had spouses, the men had jobs, they all had a vehicle, and all the children had moms and dads. Mamaw and I had not one of these things. Mamaw and I were not accepted; we were not a fit; we were not suited, and we had no place in their church society or group. They treated us as underclass, poor, having personal failure, and they subjected us to humiliations each and every time they passed us walking to church. Not offering us a ride to church was the proof of their strong feelings of disapproval. They were treating us with the contempt they thought we deserved. Mamaw was just a poor old woman trying to raise an unwanted grandchild. She worked so hard and long hours, never asking for or receiving help from anyone. I cry when I think of her sacrifice and her doing without because she wanted me to have things like other children.

There is never a reason for anyone to act or think they are better than someone else. That arrogant opinion is never accepted or excused.

Mamaw always told me to never be lukewarm in anything. She always said to be passionate and to always be 100 percent engaged, giving my all to God, family, work, and all other matters in my life. To stand and hold firm in all situations, always making sure I am standing on the side of right and truth. People who live lukewarm lives are indifferent with no passion, no vision, and no purpose. They are satisfied to just go along and never have much to contribute. Their heart and soul will only hold half of what it should. Their heart will be cold. Lukewarm people will choose what will gain them friends, power, and money over what is right; they care most about what people think of them and wanting to fit in. The lukewarm Christian will only allow God to be involved in their life part of the time. Lukewarm people may not serve a great purpose in the church. The church my Mamaw worshipped in and revered had grown to be lukewarm. Her church was self-delusional.

A church that validated evidence of being self-delusional by its persistent obnoxious, unwelcome, and offensive conduct toward us. And no one came forward to admit and call attention to the little reverence being given toward God. They all allowed me and Mamaw to walk to and from church, 2½ miles one way, every service rain or shine. We did this for years. Mamaw finally came to the realization she must free me and her from the only church that ever held her membership. She would leave behind the good and the bad memories of her church. Mamaw would never look back on her decision to leave. Mamaw had given her decision careful long thought and prayer. She was confident and satisfied with her conclusion. Mamaw felt she had been candid, used sound judgment, and been fair and sensible with her evaluation. She forgave the church for their self-righteous behavior shown toward her and her young granddaughter. However, this in no way meant she should or that she would allow this exhibit of deliberate humiliation directed toward us to continue. Enough was enough. Mamaw would execute her decision. Mamaw left her church, and she did so, holding her head high!

The new church grandmother and I attended was a blessing. My Mamaw was a woman of strong faith. She was a spirited woman with bold courage. I always remember her being obedient to God's word. What a wonderful blessing God gave this abandoned baby girl when he placed her in the arms of her Mamaw. This was his perfect plan.

9

Uncle Ben, in Love with Money

My grandparents had a son, Uncle Ben. He was three years older than Mother. Until about the age of twenty-six years, Uncle Ben was an obedient son. He was a good son. He loved his family, and this was revealed through the relationship they shared. It was Uncle Ben and Mamaw who cried, begged, and pleaded with Mother not to sign my adoption papers. Uncle Ben promised Mother if she would keep me, he would help with my raising. Uncle Ben was a senior in high school when I was born.

When Grandfather, my Papaw, passed away, Ben went to live with Pa and Aunt Lottie. Now, I was with Uncle Ben every day until he left for the army to fight in the Korean War. He had a job and helped my Mamaw support me. He loved his family and loved helping them. This is who he was back then.

Pa, Uncle Ben's grandfather, was his ideal man. He spent a lot of time with Pa when he was little. Pa had a green thumb, and he had Uncle Ben growing roses and award-winning tomatoes at eight years old. Ben also grew to know a green thumb. He and Pa could grow anything in the rich Illinois dirt.

Uncle Ben always had a loving and respectful relationship with his mother and dad, my grandparents. Like everyone, he tried to get along with his sister, my mother. Of course, their relationship was continuous. There was hostility, anger, aggression, and much jealousy directed at Uncle Ben. Mother was always a very jealous person inflicting sadness on everyone. Mother could be awarded first place ribbon in the use of profanity and slurs. Ben's choice of friends met with his parents' approval. However, Mother's choice of friends did not. She always chose friends of declining, crumbling, and decaying character. She met my dad while being in the company of such individuals.

My dad and his family never got in trouble with the law. They were just a bunch of undisciplined fun and noise-makers. Their greatest achievement was hosting a carefree and sometimes wild party. My dad was young and misguided. Most of his decisions in his youth were based on poor judgment and inconsiderate, uncaring thought. He acted on impulse, granting his desires. These irresponsible actions carried out by Dad most often resulted in mistakes with undesirable consequences.

Uncle Ben was not confrontational like Mother. He was known by family and friends as never using profanity or telling a dirty joke. He worked odd jobs through middle school and high school. Uncle Ben never got into trouble. He did not cause grandparents worry, anxiety, or stress. Ben started out his young life resembling and displaying many of the same qualities and characteristics of his grandfather, Pa. It appeared Ben had a good heart filled with kindness, consideration, generosity, and compassion for family and his fellow man. Later in life, Ben changed. He became weak and he became a follower. He would follow the instruction, demands, and wishes of someone whose core values were much different from those of Ben's family, different from the values Ben was taught and witnessed growing up.

I remember Uncle Ben being good to me and his mother, Mamaw, in the early years. He bought me a tricycle, snow sled, and a red wagon. Shortly after he was married, he gave me a kitten and a beautiful rabbit. He was hugs and kisses. I loved him very much. I thought he hung the moon. This expression meant I thought of Uncle Ben with overwhelming admiration and love.

However, everything about Ben's relationship with his family changed shortly after his marriage. Upon his return from the army, he married Joan. Aunt Joan lived in a big white house with an upstairs. Once Uncle Ben took me to Aunt Joan's house when they were dating. She was very pretty. I remember seeing her come down the long stairs to greet Uncle Ben. I thought she looked like a beautiful princess.

Now married for a short time, Ben's attitude and relationship toward his family began to change drastically. Remember he was nonconfrontational and would seldom offer a defense. He always lacked showing authority and always strived for agreement and harmony. He liked to be calm using diplomacy when dealing with situations. He tried to keep peace and avoid hurt feelings with his neutral approach. Something was happening. Ben was giving the appearance he no longer had the desire to have a connection to the family he had once given his love and respect.

My Papaw worked for Alcoa until his death. Growing up, Uncle Ben and Mother had what most everyone did whose dad worked in the mines. They received a good standard of living in comparison to other Rosiclare families. But by no means would you consider my grandparents to have money. Uncle Ben's dad, my Papaw, worked hard and provided well for his family; however, he and Uncle Ben's mother, my Mamaw, still had to remain frugal and thrifty with their income.

Uncle Ben married into a family with money and assets. They liked Ben and were very generous with him and Aunt Joan, their daughter, throughout their married life. Ben had left a family with only enough money to support themselves with a modest lifestyle. His marriage to Joan had given him the peace of never needing to be concerned about having enough money. This new family, their comfortable way of life, and their influence in the town they lived went to Uncle Ben's head. He became ashamed of his family. He was no longer the Ben his family knew. Ben would never return to the teaching and the example of his humble upbringing. He now bragged, exaggerated, and revealed to his widowed mother, Mamaw, an uncomfortable and disengaged attitude. It became very obvious his new family was his only family.

Mamaw asked Uncle Ben only one time for money or help. She asked for $20 to go to the doctor. When Ben told her he would have to ask Aunt Joan, Mamaw told him to forget the $20. Mamaw was always self-reliant, strongly independent, and capable. I never knew my Mamaw to ask or rely on another for money, emotional support, or help of any kind. She was a person who liked and respected herself. She trusted her judgment and never asked for opinions when making decisions. She had great confidence in her relationship with Jesus Christ. She knew he kept his promises. She handed to him her problems, her struggles, and her many challenges. God never disappointed her. She had little but she always had enough.

Mamaw never asked Uncle Ben to help with me. She knew he was responsible to his family of Aunt Joan and their two little boys. But to our surprise, Ben's disgust, resentment, bitterness, and anger of the fact she was raising me frequently was declared and expressed. I observed on many occasions when Ben would tell Mamaw he would never give her as little as a dime. He would also tell grandmother the reason for his decision. The reason he gave was she was spending it on supporting me. If Mamaw did not take me to raise, who did Uncle Ben think would? He and Aunt Joan would not. My dad and his proven to be very jealous wife would not. My mother did not want me. Pa and Aunt Lottie could not financially, emotionally, or physically raise me. There was no one but Mamaw to care for me.

All my family—except for Mamaw, Pa, and Aunt Lottie—ignored me. They all made me feel isolated and alone. My extended family made me feel like I did not belong. They regarded me as something that was in the way and of no value or importance. None of the family liked my dad. They never wanted to be associated with mother because she was always rebellious, causing conflict in the family. They considered my dad no good and mother an unmanageable trouble-making person. Since I was their offspring, I was considered and treated like an outcast. This treatment of my family added much harm and sadness to my already broken heart and spirit. I learned early in my young life I would never be able to change the hearts and minds of my extended family. The memory of their hostility is still present. I always thought I was in a crowd of people with no person seeing me or acknowledging me. I was always made to feel like a nobody. Even today the damage done to me as a child by insensitive people still continues to haunt me and exist in my life. These emotional problems brought on by the abandonment of our parents are deep-rooted. They will remain alive, continue to persist, and try to keep our life from being happy. The problems our parents caused will decline in magnitude, and they will weaken with time. We will learn to manage these problems. We will dominate them. They will not dominate us. Our unconventional start in life will make us stronger. We will be determined. We will be unimpressed, impervious, and never persuaded by the wrong and destructive influence of others. We have already experienced the approval of others is not a requisite for our existence and the life we will make for ourselves.

Uncle Ben knew his actions toward his family were wrong. He was weak, ineffective, incapable, and powerless to defend what was right. He had accepted Joan's demands. His behavior toward his family was unconscionable, and he was disgraceful for not correcting it. Uncle Ben never had the capability and the willingness to return as the loving, caring, reasoning son of his mother. His show of no compassion and the embarrassment he felt for his family was like an incurable disease. Uncle Ben had loved me and wanted a good life for me in my early childhood. Then one day when I was somewhere around eight years old, without warning, he would fail to even acknowledge I was in the room. In Ben's mind, heart, soul, and conscience, I no longer existed. He fell prey to the influence of Joan and her family's money and their control of him.

Unlike Ben's new family, our family, and now Uncle Ben's old family had no influence, no money, and no control. Our family was considered to be poor. Ben's dad, Papaw, had passed away, meaning no more Alcoa job. Pa was on a fixed income, and Aunt Lottie was incapable of earning money. Mamaw's only income was washing and ironing for people, and I was the needy and helpless child. Uncle Ben considered this shameful and embarrassing. There is nothing shameful about hard work. Nothing shameful about being honest, kind, and showing respect to others. Nothing shameful about making it on your own no matter how modest and simple your life. God does not care about your life's quantity. God cares about your life's quality. Nothing shameful about not taking handouts from the government or from anywhere. I have never been ashamed of those three old people. I am proud of them. They all three took on the big responsibility of raising a child nobody wanted. I should not have become their burden. They were not obligated to raise me. I will always acknowledge the fact they loved and wanted me. They gave me a Christian environment that would influence my life. Mamaw, Pa, and Aunt Lottie will live in my heart and mind forever. They will always be that small inner voice I hear when I need love and strength. God's ways are perfect. He was not going to allow me being without the love of a mother and dad destroy the plan he had for my life.

Yes, we were poor in the sight of others. Everyone thought of us as poor. Mamaw, Pa, and Aunt Lottie's poor held no weight, no importance, no significance, and its value amounted to nothing according to Ben. People and Ben were wrong. These three old people were not poor. They were rich. Their wealth was not material wealth. It was their faith in God. Unlike Ben, the wealth of those three old people would never be lost or left behind. Ben had forgotten the teaching of his family. He would never come to know his family had the wealth. His family had eternal wealth. God wants us to prosper. He wants us to have money to supply ourselves and our family's needs. He desires us to be willing and able to give and share with those less fortunate. There is nothing wrong with money as long as it is kept in perspective. We need to give to the church, enabling them to continue to be witnesses of God's word. God understands we need money to survive and enjoy the life he yearns for us. God wants us to have money. He just does not want money to have us.

You have heard the old saying money cannot buy happiness. This is true. There are many things in life money cannot buy. I am going to mention some of them; however, I am sure you know of more. Money cannot buy time, eternal life with Jesus, salvation, health, peace, character, respect, common sense, love, patience, integrity, forgiveness, morals, compassion, generosity, kindness, true friends, intelligence to name a few. Happy times with loved ones and family can touch a heart and fill a soul in a way that money cannot compete. My Mamaw left a legacy of love and wisdom. Some people in Rosiclare treated her adversely because she was poor. But they respected her. They knew of the Christian life she lived. My mother left a legacy of pain and suffering. My dad left a legacy of neglect and glaring contemptuous disregard for his little girl. Uncle Ben left a legacy of greed and selfishness. I do not know if he ever learned knowing Jesus held more value than money. My honest account of these individuals should make all of us careful with our words and our actions. Our words and our actions will be remembered in the legacy we leave. They will be remembered long after we are gone.

The end of Uncle Ben's life was tragic. His mother and dad, Mamaw and Papaw, raised him in church. He stopped attending church in his early teenage years. Ben never accepted Jesus as his savior until maybe the very end of his life. I recall on many occasions, his mother's, Mamaw's, prayers for Ben's salvation. I observed her tell Ben many, many times one day he would fall, and that fall would be hard. Because you understand, Uncle Ben felt he did not need God in his life.

Uncle Ben never had an automobile accident. He never got a speeding ticket. He was less than a mile from his home when a young man caused a traffic accident that took Ben's life and seriously injured Joan. A year prior to this deadly vehicle collision, one of Ben's sons passed away because of a blood clot to his heart. The remaining child, a son, was hurt in a mining accident and is now disabled.

A minister in their small town came upon the wreck involving Uncle Ben and Joan. This minister rode to the hospital in the ambulance with Ben. He stayed with Ben and witnessed to him until Ben succumbed. The minister told us Ben was conscious when he accepted Jesus as his savior, and then he quietly slipped away. This same minister presided over Ben's funeral. He shared with the family the last few minutes of Ben's life. He also shared with the family what he believed to be Ben's salvation. I wonder if Ben at the end of his life was remembering his mother's warning. The warning of the hard fall he would one day receive if he continued to live his life without Jesus. I feel grandmother's prayers were answered that day. God sent the minister to Ben giving him one last chance. We believe Uncle Ben accepted Jesus. Ben was eighty years old when he departed from this life.

Ben's heart had been hardened for so long. Calluses had grown on his heart and conscience. He could no longer see, hear, or feel the truth. Ben was now being controlled, led by what fed his hungry insatiable appetite. The appetite for money and status. He now took his command, his life's orders from his best friends. Ben's best friends would be called pride, arrogance, ego, and greed.

Never will surrender bring victory except in surrendering your life to Jesus.

10

To Everyone, He Was Uncle John, but to me, He Was Pa

Everyone in Rosiclare knew and loved Uncle John. He was admired and respected by all. Unlike me and Mamaw, he was never looked down on or forgotten by the town's elitist or the town's want to be elitist. He was a very good and kind man. He was treated so well by the entire town in some measure because all Rosiclare knew what Alcoa thought of Uncle John. That, in part, helped to make him admired, held in high esteem, adulated, and revered.

Uncle John, my Pa, was never critical of anyone. Always willing to help anyone in need, sharing anything he possessed. I never in sixteen years of living with him heard him raise his voice or speak an unkind word. He was always of good cheer and lived every day being happy. If he was ever discouraged or worried, he never let it be known. His dirty word when he was perplexed or displeased was goodness gracious. I witnessed him saying goodness gracious to a great extent growing up. Every time Pa picked up the hammer he would hit his thumb. Goodness gracious was heard a lot around my house when I was a little girl. Pa's lack of skill and coordination with a hammer was not comical. Carpentry was not one of his many talents.

Earlier I told you Mamaw and I moved in with great-grandfather, Pa, and Great-Aunt Lottie. Pa was Mamaw's widowed father and Aunt Lottie was Mamaw's old maid sister. After my Papaw passed away, moving in and making our home with those two old family members was a blessing—a good decision. I went to live with them. I was twenty-one months old.

Mamaw cooked, did laundry, cleaned, canned garden vegetables, and helped with Aunt Lottie. This helped her feel like she was paying her and my debt to Pa for allowing us to live in his home. Pa loved us being there. He lived for his family. Pa was only fifty-four years old when his wife, the mother of his seven children, passed away. He never remarried and never had a date or girlfriend. He always found joy in the simple things of life. Pa read his bible often. He read the weekly newspaper every Thursday. He read that newspaper whose content was sharing the happenings of Hardin County. He read it cover to cover not missing a word.

Pa loved working in his yard and his garden. He also loved mine and his best friend, our dog Dover. Pa, Dover, and me went on many walks together. My great-grandfather was a humble man. Pa was kind, helpful, and he was respectful to everyone. He and my husband, Gary, were the kindest men I have ever known. Throughout Pa's life he was selfless. He was always more concerned with the needs and desires of others than concern for himself. He was a wise old man. He was unconditionally and totally generous and charitable with his time, energy, loyalty, and responsibility. He was of good nature; however, he would never allow being taken advantage of. Only if needed, Pa would be generous with what little money he had. One neighbor, who was an executive with Alcoa borrowed money often. He always paid it back. It was not much money. Pa did not have much money. However, $20 or $30 in those days would buy a lot. The only people who ever knew about the prominent Alcoa employee borrowing money from Pa were those three old people. Mamaw and Aunt Lottie would probably not have known but the man always came to our house to ask for the money.

My Mamaw always told me it is not what you make but what you save. This is true. This neighbor's income was exceedingly greater than Pa's. We had very little money, but it was enough. It was enough because we never demanded or craved the finer worldly things in life. We always lived within our means. We never spent more than we could afford. Pa and Mamaw never borrowed money. We lived a life of simplicity and we were not self-indulgent. Pa was never impressed by possession and status. He could always give you a reason to be hopeful and positive. He knew what was important in life.

Pa's heart was kind, sincere, pure, and filled with love. Love for God, his family, and his fellow man. Pa spoke with candor and acted with integrity. He was a simple man with no skill, no wealth, no education, but he was loved and revered by everyone who knew him. In Hardin County, he was revered by people who did not know him personally but knew of him because of his relationship and reputation with Alcoa.

Pa retired from Alcoa in Rosiclare. Alcoa owned many houses in Rosiclare in which their employees could rent for themselves and their families to live and make their home. My best friend, Carole's family, rented an Alcoa house as most all Alcoa employees. Pa was the only Alcoa employee after retirement that was given an Alcoa-owned house to live in. They gave Pa their house rent-free, with utilities free, until his death at age ninety-six. I lived in that Alcoa-owned house for sixteen years of my life, leaving Rosiclare after high school graduation. Pa only received a small monthly retirement check from Alcoa and a small Social Security check, totaling $123 a month. Pa provided Mamaw and me a place to live, utilities, and food. Alcoa knew Mamaw washed and ironed for a living so she could provide for me, but they never made Pa pay for any utilities. Anything Alcoa did to their other houses, they provided the same for Pa. When Alcoa installed running water and a bathroom in their houses, we got running water and a bathroom too.

Once a year, the out-of-town Alcoa executives would come to Rosiclare for their big annual business meeting. The evening before they returned home was spent at the Rosiclare Hotel, enjoying a fine dinner and smoking cigars. Every year, a big, long black Cadillac would drive in front of our house. Alcoa had come to take Pa to dinner with the company executives. No other company employee received that honor, and no other employee was shown the appreciation given to my great-grandfather. In all Alcoa did for Pa, they had to have tremendous respect and gratitude for him. Pa was only a common laborer with no title and no education. Alcoa never bestowed favors and appreciation of that extent to any other employee of their Hardin County mining operation except great-grandfather, who had only a third-grade education. What Alcoa did for him, they did not extend to any other employee. The honorary treatment Alcoa afforded Pa speaks volumes about their opinion of him. Pa had integrity, always staying on the side of truth, and he made ethical decisions in all circumstances. He lived a life free from bias and external pressure, making decisions with a clear mind and without emotion. Pa's mind stayed clear, sensible, and wise to a very old age. A few months prior to his death, he declined cognitively. Pa was always the gentle man and a friend to everyone.

At one time, Rosiclare had a fluorspar museum, and there you could find pictures of Pa, Uncle John sitting at a long dinner table with Alcoa executives, enjoying dinner and cigars.

All the money Pa received each month was his Alcoa pension and Social Security. Alcoa's pension was not much, but it was comparable to other large companies at that time, and even years later, their pension was not substantial. They were a good company to work for, providing financial security to Rosiclare.

Every Christmas, Alcoa would have a Christmas party for the children of their employees. They would have Santa Claus, songs, lots of candy, drinks, cake, ice cream, nuts, and a wide variety and selection of fruits. Every child in attendance received a nice gift, with gifts varying according to the child's age. Alcoa was charitable to these children with their Christmas party, always having a huge decorated Christmas tree. All Alcoa families, meaning employees, spouse, and children were invited. Great-grandfather and I received an invitation to the Christmas party. Pa and I went every year to Alcoa's big Christmas party. I came home with the same gift as every other girl of approximately the same age as me. I was so proud of my Pa. The Alcoa party for employees and their children was a very big deal in Rosiclare, and of course, Pa was the only retiree invited, and I was the only great-grandchild invited. To this day, I do not know why Alcoa favored and gifted my great-grandfather. He was a very humble and simple man, but they showed much more respect and loyalty to Pa than to any other employee. Pa was special.

My family never wanted money from anywhere unless they worked and earned it. They also believed in taking care of your responsibility. I remember on two different occasions individuals from the government office knocked on our door. They told Pa he could receive financial assistance for his daughter, Great-Aunt Lottie. Aunt Lottie was marginally mentally challenged. She was a little slow, not educated, and incapable of holding down a job and earning money. I witnessed on both occasions Pa graciously declining their offer. He did not invite them into the house to explain. Pa told the men Aunt Lottie was his responsibility and thanked them for their concern and generosity. Pa would never have accepted a check from the government for the care and support of Aunt Lottie. He considered this charity, and my family did not accept charity.

Every Christmas he and I would look for a Christmas tree. We lived in front of the railroad tracks, and behind the tracks was a big wooded area. Pa, Dover, and I always found a beautiful tree. He would cut it down, and I would help him carry it home. Christmas was a real special time. It was the only time we had nuts, candy, or fruit in the house. Our food budget did not make room for these extras. I was the only great-grandchild who got a Christmas present from Pa. Every Christmas, as far back as I can remember, he would give me one dollar for Christmas. He would always ask if I wanted the change or the dollar bill. When I was little, I always wanted the change because the coins looked like more money than receiving the dollar bill. Even after I was grown, Pa would continue to give me one dollar at Christmas. It's those little things that said "I love you." I was twenty years old and working, but Pa still gave me my one-dollar Christmas gift. He remembered when one dollar was considered a decent amount of money. Remember, I was the only great-grand-child to ever receive a Christmas gift from Pa. But I was the only great-grandchild he helped to raise. Today, that one-dollar Christmas gift from him is one of my most happy memories of growing up. I was always Pa's little girl, and I had no one but those three old people. I gave their life purpose, and we all needed each other.

A carnival came to town when I was seven years old. Pony rides were 25¢ each. Pa gave me two quarters to ride the ponies. I remember being so happy and excited. Two quarters from Pa made me happy and made me feel loved. I remember being sick with a bad cold one winter. I had a cough and a fever, and I wanted chicken noodle soup. Pa walked to town in the cold and snow to get me a can of soup. Downtown Rosiclare was at least one and a half miles away, and maybe a little more. My family was accustomed to the walk, and Pa never got sick. Not once do I remember him or Aunt Lottie ailing in health. I only remember my grandmother one time not feeling well when she needed $20 to go to the doctor.

We always had a big yard, and the lawn mower was a push mower. Pa kept the blades on the mower sharp, and I always mowed the grass for him. He never asked or told me to, I just always loved gardening, the outdoors, and spending time with Pa.

Everyone had gasoline-powered mowers but us. I never thought of being poor when I was growing up in Rosiclare. Maybe that was another one of God's protections.

We had a big, ugly potbelly cast-iron coal-burning stove in the living room, and it was the only means of heating the house in the winter. The living room was the only room in the house that was warm in the cold months. Pa was up at five o'clock every morning in the winter, reloading the coal stove. Every morning, my Mamaw would put a big pot of beans on top of the coal stove. She would cook them all day and season them with fatback. This made the beans delicious, and I loved to drink bean soup. She always made sure there was a lot of bean soup. We had beans every meal, both winter and summer. Today, one of my favorite meals is beans seasoned with fatback, onion, fried potatoes, and cornbread. Beans were both healthy for us and cheap, and no one ever had health issues from the greasy fried potatoes and fatback. In fact, all three of them lived healthy into their eighties and nineties. Maybe all the hard work, walking everywhere they went, and beans helped keep them healthy.

With only a third-grade education, Pa read his Bible almost every day. He managed his garden by the Farmer's Almanac. He and I always had a big garden, and he followed the instructions of the Farmer's Almanac down to the smallest detail. He enjoyed gardening immensely and always had one of the best gardens around. Pa could grow anything in his garden, and he always planted watermelons for me. I was spoiled but in a good way. I certainly did not get a lot of what I desired. Maybe I should say I was nurtured, not spoiled. I never talked hatefully to them. I obeyed their every word and respected them so much. I was equally proud of them. Nothing could make me defy or challenge their authority. I was little and did not know there was no reason for me to worry. I was a child that worried a lot, but there was nothing for me to worry about. Those three old people kept everything good. Pa knew that happiness and satisfaction with your life are found in the love, respect, and relationship you have with family, work, friends, and Jesus. Pa was poor when it came to money and material things, but if respect had any value, he was undoubtedly the wealthiest man in Rosiclare. He was the family rock for many years, and everyone in Rosiclare called him Uncle John.

I had a very simple life growing up in Rosiclare, but I had three people who loved me, cared for me, and protected me. They were not my mother and dad, but somehow I learned not to be too sad for what is over and done, but to look forward and never look back. Times change, but the harm done to a child by parents who abandon them does not. We learn to deal with the emotions caused by their betrayal. We are not alone on this journey, as many children have been left by their parents. We will survive with a bold existence resulting in courage, purpose, confidence, and living wisely. They made us special, unique, important, and winners, and their abandonment has made us determined to challenge ourselves to live a meaningful life. While growing up, when I was at home in the company of Mamaw, Pa, and Aunt Lottie, the echoing of my laughter was ever present. I was blessed.

I hope you will find a family member, friend, teacher, neighbor, employer, anyone who will be a good mentor to you, a trusted advisor who will guide, support, motivate, and teach you to be wise in all you do and say, helping you to discover your God-given talent and use it to your potential, as we all have gifts and talents.

My great-grandfather was one of the most humble people I have ever known. He spent his life dedicated to the needs of his family and others, never wanting much and never getting much. He never cared for status or praise, but all over Rosiclare, he was known, respected, and loved just for being himself. He was considered to be a huge man, receiving everyone's esteem, warm approval, and heartfelt affection. He was loved by his family and the people of Rosiclare. Pa, Uncle John, will never be forgotten, and he will live in the hearts of many. The man was good all the time to everyone. Uncle John was famous in Rosiclare for his kindness, character, and reputation. All this love, respect, and admiration were not needed for him to be happy. He was happy being with and loving his family, and he was happy being a good, humble man. Pa was born in 1873 and died in 1969. Pa witnessed so many changes in the way people viewed happiness and success, but he never changed. He had it right for ninety-six years.

Pa passed away in January 1969 on a cold, drizzling, rainy Illinois day. The church could not accommodate all the people attending his funeral, and there was a long line of people standing outside the church under umbrellas. Of course, he had prepaid for his funeral and Aunt Lottie's many years earlier because he always took care of business. His funeral was big, another realization and consciousness to his family and friends as to the quality and caliber of this old man's life. He left a legacy of the finest and of the greatest humanity and brotherly love anyone in Rosiclare had ever seen or would ever see again.

Pa is in heaven, and I believe he has a beautiful garden with watermelons waiting for me. He is probably reading the latest issue of the Farmer's Almanac.

> Humble yourselves in the sight of the Lord, and
> he shall lift you up. (James 4:10 KJV)

My Good Hearted Pa

My Pa, My Aunt Lottie

11

Grand Lady, Great-Aunt Lottie

Aunt Lottie was very involved in my upbringing. She was a blessing, a sweet soul with unfailing smiles and patience, always happy and never complaining.

Aunt Lottie never married, and the only family she had was my Mamaw, Pa, and me. She was a little slow and was not made to go to school. I always doubted her being slightly mentally challenged. Without an education and being considered slow mentally, Aunt Lottie could not work and earn money, but a person could have a good conversation with her. She had the ability to clearly understand and remember things. Like the other women mentioned in this book, Aunt Lottie saw circumstances and situations for what they truly were. She saw in people characteristics that many individuals would not notice. She was wise and savvy, and her practical nature of living in reality kept her clued in with a clear view of what is most important in one's life. She would not be misled or hoodwinked; she was a tough but fair woman.

Aunt Lottie never gossiped and would tell on nobody. Aunt Joan, my little cousin Tommy's mother, often had him on a diet, and I would slip him food to eat that he was not allowed. Aunt Lottie on many occasions saw this, and she never said a word about it to anyone.

Aunt Lottie kissed away my tears, my cuts and bruises, and she rocked me to sleep many nights. She thought everything I did or said was cute. Her pride, joy, purpose, and love were all wrapped up for me. To be honest, she spoiled me, but those three old people did not care to correct me when I misbehaved, and Aunt Lottie was no exception. If I did something wrong, I need not look to Aunt Lottie for sympathy, but if I ever needed defending, she was always available with a powerful defense. She was another woman who influenced my life with her steadfast unwavering love and protection for me. Her allegiance to me was dependable and loyal until the day she died. I loved that lady.

Aunt Lottie loved Juicy Fruit chewing gum. So many times she would have only one piece left, and she would always give it to me. I drank a lot of whole milk, and Aunt Lottie would taste the milk for me to make sure it was fresh and not souring. If the milk passed the test, I would then drink a glass.

Aunt Lottie had thick, coarse red hair. When I was little, she would let me play beauty shop with her hair. I would roll, tease, comb, and pull. If I pulled her hair, she would let me know with a giggle. I painted her nails and put loads of makeup on her. Everything I ever did as a child or an adult met with her approval.

Every year, my Mamaw and I would walk to her church for their Christmas Eve service. When we returned home, Santa had been to my house and left my Christmas gifts under the tree. Aunt Lottie had put all the gifts out and told me Santa had delivered them. Of course, Mamaw had bought everything with the money she made washing and ironing laundry for those four families. There was nothing from my dad or any member of his family. I am sure I had as good a Christmas as anyone. I would receive a small gift from my mother. She did most always remember me at Christmas and birthdays, and

I would receive a token gift from Uncle Ben and Aunt Joan only at Christmas. They never gave me a birthday gift, graduation gift, or a wedding gift. I never once in my life received or was given a gift, card, or phone call from my dad for birthdays or Christmas. I often wondered if he ever was concerned or even interested enough to want to know what kind of Christmas his little girl would have to enjoy. I think it is undeniably fair to say he was not the least troubled or occupied with such a thought.

When I lost a baby tooth, the tooth fairy (Mamaw) would leave a quarter under my pillow. There was always a stick of Juicy Fruit gum under my pillow too. I thought the quarter came from the tooth fairy, but I knew Aunt Lottie had placed the gum under my pillow. They all three made a big effort to ensure and make certain I did not miss out on the things that make children happy.

As a child, I was always quiet and shy. Even though I was loved very much and I knew I was loved, you could look at me and notice something was missing. I was young and happy and did not realize until I was older the reason I always had a sad look in my eyes. What was missing was the love and relationship a child longs for with their mother and dad. Some children will suffer more damage than others from the abusive neglect of their parents. Because of my passive, unresisting, obedient, and subdued nature, I was unfortunately one of those children who suffered immensely. Mamaw, Pa, and Aunt Lottie never discussed my parents. You will read later in the book how I did very well without them. The purpose of this book is to show you the life you have been given is as important as anyone's. You were meant to have a life to be proud of. You were meant to leave a legacy of noble character with long-lasting actions and personality traits to be emulated and carried forward to family and friends. You will like yourself. You will hold your head up high.

Aunt Lottie's gentle way was in view and easily recognizable to anyone who met her. She also was humble. Her fame was being a grand lady who loved and stood united with her family. Aunt Lottie was unassuming with no desire for attention. She was always smiling. A smile makes people happy. Your smile is free. It does not cost you time or money. It can often change the attitude of someone. Aunt Lottie's smiles were warm and genuine. No pretense, for she was exactly as she appeared.

I know there had to be concerns of raising a little child, but they never let it be known. If something had happened to Pa, the free use of the Alcoa house and utilities would cease to exist. The uncertainty of this perhaps happening had to cross their mind. My Mamaw was of resolute character and did not quit or give up. She would have found a solution. Thankfully, she did not have this challenge for years after I graduated, and I left home. God's plan for all three of them was a long healthy life. I was placed in that home for a reason. I gave them purpose and a goal. They gave me the chance for a wonderful life I would never get from anyone else in my family. I was expected to mind and to be good. Even as a little girl, I never wanted to disappoint them. Caring for me was a great sacrifice. Even though we always struggled financially, there was always just enough. I captured their heart. They were protecting my future, giving me stability and devotion. No matter the circumstances. They all three stayed grounded to their core values and beliefs. Making wise decisions and never losing their hope, plan, and vision for my destiny. I will always give my love, respect, and gratitude to them for my blessed life. I will always remember my roots. I will always remember the effort, trials, toil, and struggles they diligently went through to be faithful to God's plan. My parents were so selfish and despicable, handing the burden of raising me to these poor and old people. They all three showered me with love. They did not raise their voice in anger. There was respect and harmony in that home.

When I think about or read the following scripture, it reminds me of the three people who raised me. They all kept charging full speed ahead, completing their mission. They had no money. They had no way of making money other than Mamaw's $20 a week doing laundry and Pa's monthly income of $123. They did not possess or experience things of high quality or luxury. They had nothing costing money considered to be pretty, comfortable, elegant, enjoyable, and self-indulgent. They had all the riches they wanted. They had each other, me, friends, health, love, and respect. None of the riches they had were commodities to purchase. Maybe this is why I have always been low maintenance. Being low maintenance is a compliment and financial protection.

> Fear thou not, for I am with thee: be not dismayed, for I am thy God: I will strengthen thee; yea, I will help thee; yea, I will uphold thee with the right hand of my righteousness. (Isaiah 41:10 KJV)

Aunt Lottie encouraged me and helped me when I looked and felt weak. She knew I was hurting. She knew my mother and dad. She understood it all, and she showed so much patience to this little girl. She knew I had been abandoned, betrayed by my parents' lack of love, support, and total neglect.

She understood the damage my parents did would translate into lifelong psychological consequences. Aunt Lottie realized there was nothing she could do to fix the harm parents had caused, but she continued to console me. Sometimes she probably thought I was inconsolable. But she was always there, showering me with the little things in life that let a child know they are loved. Her best two little things were smiles and hugs. Lots of memorable times spent with Aunt Lottie. God turns these little things in your life into big things. These little things God made big had consequential meaning and lasting effect on my future. I am thankful for the love put in my Aunt Lottie's heart. I am so blessed God put Aunt Lottie in my life so she could shower me with her love.

Aunt Lottie lived to be ninety-eight years of age. Aunt Lottie served her family well. She was a beautiful gift and blessing to me. She was a loving, devoted, and loyal aunt. Her wants and needs were near to nothing. Always giving and never asking or receiving. She left a wonderful memory. The legacy Aunt Lottie left to me was much wealth of love and the exemplification of a godly lady.

You will learn about the good people I devote a chapter. Kindness was always in their heart and on their lips. They gave me their love by showing me kindness. They all were selfless and their spirit showed me they stayed in step with Jesus. I saw every day faith, hope, love, courage, and character. I witnessed every day through each of them what having a relationship with Jesus Christ does to the soul. Even as a youth, I came to realize their soul held great value. All these wonderful people God put in my young life are still in my life today. Be kind to everyone. Give a smile, say a kind word, be of service to others. Kindness can influence, change, and shape a life. My life was shaped, was molded by the kindness shared with me by these good people in my youth. Their memory will never be absent in my heart.

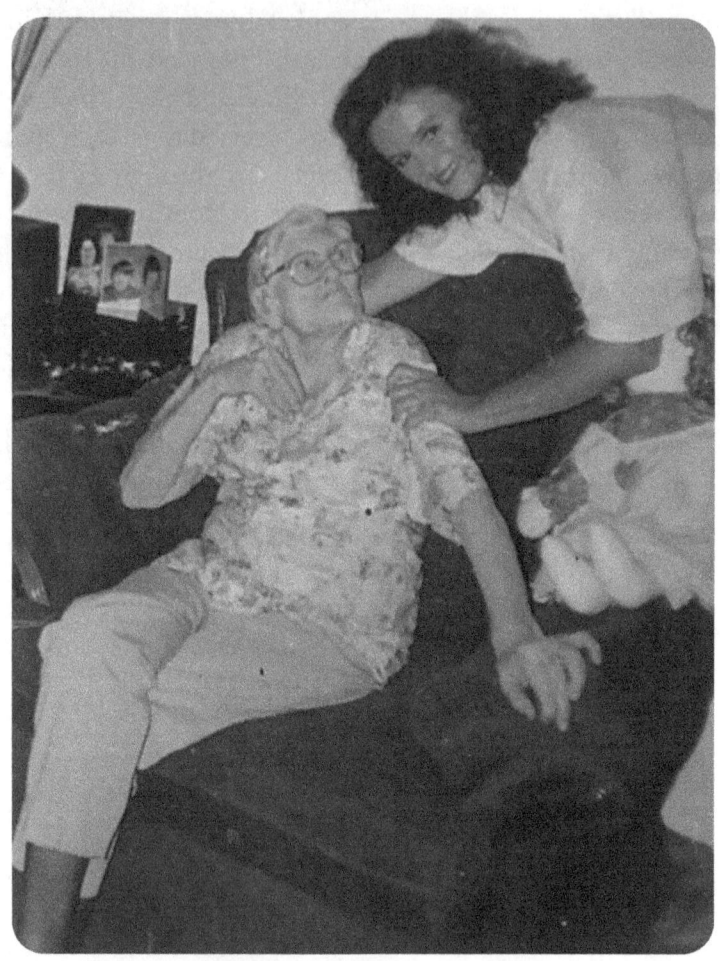

Me and Gracious Aunt Lottie

12

My Home Away from Home

Growing up in Rosiclare, I knew I was loved in two homes. My home and my friend Carole's home. Her family was an important and giant positive influence in my parenting and child rearing. Carole was an only child. I was also alone. We became close friends, close as sisters, and still are today. Carole's mother, Hazel, and her dad, Harold, were special people.

One of the many reasons Carole's parents were special was they cared. Carole's mother and dad were each other's inspiration. Enveloping each other and Carole with protection and love. They created a supportive and loving home allowing Carole to mature to adulthood with confidence in her abilities and talents. She knew her parents' love and commitment to her would never weaken or vanish regardless of the number of passing years.

Hazel, Carole's Mother

She openeth her mouth with wisdom; and in her tongue is the law of kindness. (Proverbs 31:26 KJV)

I sometimes think Mamaw and Hazel compared their notes and lessons on parenting. Like Mamaw, Hazel was an authoritative parent. Neither of these two ladies superficially made any wrong acceptable. Carole and I always knew we would be held accountable, and discipline for us would turn out badly for failing to obey them. We understand now their reasoning behind this decision when we showed a defiant attitude. Hazel knew brazen, insubordinate, and ignored disobedient behavior would cause Carole to develop unfavorable character and personality habits and traits. Hazel and Mamaw were conscious of the truth. They realized their actions of holding me and Carole accountable for not obeying them would build and develop important virtues.

These virtues would give us the temperament to take the initiative and react with prudence, wisdom, and good shrewd common-sense judgment. This lesson on accountability building virtues would inspire and be a guide to us in our adult years. Carole was a child like me. She seldom disobeyed her parents. The hardly ever time she disobeyed would always prove to be minuscule and insignificant. But Hazel would still hold her accountable. Hazel and Mamaw's eyes were wide open always. We did not know at our young age or did we care, but the discipline of Hazel and Mamaw was love. They were building a good future for the children they cherished and were devoted to.

Like all good mothers, Hazel kept her thumb on Carole those early childhood years. She was fixated on adhering to rules, regulations, and boundaries. She held reasonable goals and expectations for Carole. Hazel was a woman of influence. You knew to conform to her authority because you had no other choice. She established a code of values for Carole. Her words were compelling and persuasive. Her life by example was a devout Christian. Hazel's goal for Carole was to grow up to be an accomplished woman with more opportunities, more happiness, more purpose in her life than even Hazel could imagine. Like everything else, this determined woman strived toward her goal with energy, passion, effort, certainty, work, and faith. Hazel pursued her goal for Carole's life. She continued on a straight path never wavering. She was patient. This was her pledge and priority, and her confidence grew every day with optimistic vision. Hazel's goal was accomplished for Carole, and I am sure God gave his official approval.

Hazel was a positive thinking person. She brought hopefulness and sureness to Carole. Hazel was resilient. She was effervescent and would bounce back very swiftly from a difficult situation. She acted with bubbly energy adapting well in times of difficulty. Her resilience helped her handle and cope. She knew life would have its bad days, but she also knew good days were closer than you think. Hazel could always see the light when life was at its darkest. Her strong faith, optimism, coupled with her hopeful nature brought peace and comfort to her family and friends. Thoughts and attitude manage and guide our future days. Hazel made sure her thoughts and attitude were rosy and bright. They were encouraging, reassuring, heartening, and overflowing with promise. She did not allow negative thoughts and attitude to squander, waste, and devour her days. She knew how you think is who you are. And it is how other people perceive you to be. People would never see or hear Hazel discouraged, complaining, accusing, disapproving, and promoting doom and gloom. Hazel was very capable. She did correct difficult and awkward problems in her life. She did not focus on them to the extent they kept her from having happy days and a positive hopeful attitude. Hazel was a virtuous woman. She was a woman who lived her faith. People saw Hazel through her words, behavior, and her sincere Godly actions. She led her family with dignity and honor. She was not judgmental of anyone for any reason. She was kind and compassionate. However, Hazel did have a direct and sometimes blunt way of telling you the truth but never hurting your feelings, never breaking your spirit. She had a way of making you admit your mistake and at the same time helped to rid your pride and ask forgiveness of the individual you wronged. She inspired you to believe you can change and repair whatever difficult circumstances are obstructing your life. Hazel was a forgiving person and slow to anger. But like Mamaw, when enough was enough she placed into action the law of pass and repass.

Children need a strong mother. Also, like Mamaw, Hazel's faith was her strength. She was that shining light always showing her path so Carole could follow her footsteps. Hazel had all that was needed to be a good mother. She was tender love. She was tough love. She was self-assured the plan she had for Carole's future would be achieved with much success and happiness. She aimed high for Carole. She knew there would always be obstacles and hurdles in life. They come to everyone. But she also knew there would always be an escape. Hazel would finish her dream for Carole with a victory. She steadied herself with courage and a calm composed cool head. She was always even-tempered keeping her words, actions, and all emotions intact. Hazel knew aiming high for Carole's future would bring different events to her life. Carole would be in situations she had not faced and was not familiar. She also knew doubt, pressure, and stress are three unwelcome companions who feel obligated to tag along to impede your achievements. Hazel was fearless and would not be frightened from completing her ambition for Carole. She would not flinch. Like Mamaw, Hazel would not quit. She would not give up.

Hazel was an intelligent, beautiful, and wonderful mother. Carole's life is a constant and steadfast affirmation honoring her mother's intangible asset. This asset is Hazel's brand. It is Hazel's legacy. This mother's heart's desire and her strongest craving was for Carole to have a personal relationship with Jesus Christ. Like Mamaw did with me, Hazel began taking Carole to church at an early age, Carole's mother had a discerning heart. Her vision never became cloudy. Hazel's clever mindset, calmness, concentration, and her strong faith would quickly identify wrong. Many people never learn this character trait. Wrong will always make its home in a troubled person's life. Hazel's discerning heart gave her keen observation to people and situations. In other words, Hazel's wisdom and discerning heart could see right through a person. She could see the truth you thought was hidden forever. Carole received her mother's communication, affection, praise, and support. This was given by Hazel to Carole with the love and devotion only a mother can understand. Hazel was ever pleasant and the pristine perfect mom. She always dressed classy, wearing makeup, and semi–high-heel shoes.

After I was grown, Hazel shared a story of me and Carole when we were little. She said it was one of her favorite memories of our childhood. I was about four and a half years old, and Carole was about three years. I had a storybook with pictures. Mamaw had read the book to me. Carole and I were sitting on her front porch when I decided to read the storybook to Carole. Of course, I could not read a lick! Hazel said every time I turned the page, my reading and my story got bigger and better. She said I would look at the pictures (that is how I read the book—ha ha) and embellish the story to the extreme. This embellishing made the storytelling so entertaining and fascinating it held three-year-old Carole's devoted attention. Carole's great amazement and wonder-struck kept her gazed in awe for a very long time. Hazel said that was an entertaining time for her as well. She also said she had thoughts and memories of that reading session and it always brings a smile to her face and leaves her with a happy heart.

Hazel bought from Mamaw a little cheap picture for $20. Remember Mamaw needed the $20 to go to the doctor. I am certain Hazel did not want the little pitcher. However, she knew Mamaw needed to see a doctor. She also knew Mamaw would not ask to borrow the money. Neither would she allow Hazel to give her the money as a gift or even as a loan. Hazel knew how proud and independent she was. Out of concern for Mamaw and not wanting to hurt her feelings or injure her self-respect, Hazel bought the trivial little pitcher for $20. That was the only way Hazel could help Mamaw so she could see the doctor. Several years ago, Hazel gave me that pitcher and shared the story behind it. I heard Uncle Ben tell Mamaw, his mother, he would have to ask Aunt Joan if he could loan her $20. I knew Mamaw went to the doctor, but I did not know where she got the money to go. God always provides and that day the provision was her neighbor and friend, Hazel. That pitcher today sits in my china cabinet. Another reminder of the struggle for my Mamaw. A reminder of these two wonderful women and the wealth of character, strength, and righteousness they both possessed. They both benefited from the quality of their friendships. They both were amazing inspiring women way ahead of their time. They were golden role models for me and Carole.

Hazel's epitome legacy is continuing every day through the life of Carole. A good legacy is the intangible. It will stand the test of time for your family and others. It is the blueprint, the design of your purposeful life. Some people think the greatest legacy to be wealth. But the greatest legacy is the intangible of character. You cannot spend, sell, give away, or forget character.

Hazel's happiness was the hope of Carole's promising future. Hazel's devotion to her child with love, training, and prayer witnessed this hope come to reality.

Hazel lived to be ninety-five years old. Before she passed away, she saw her dreams for Carole's life accelerate time and time again.

Hazel was an above and beyond ordinary mother. One great definition of love is a mother. She taught Carole to choose her passion with determination and to make living out her dreams fun. She knew if Carole did this, she would never have a job but always have a career. Standing up for what is right is courage and conviction. This is one of the attributes that make good leaders. She wanted Carole to be tenacious and persistent. She taught navigating life problems into triumphs. Hazel coached Carole on how to be a champion. Champions believe in themselves. She coached Carole to see herself with a life she would want, would live, would enjoy, and a life brimming with goodness to benefit humanity.

Keep strong faith in your self-worth. A healthy confidence is resilient in moving you forward with optimistic perseverance when life with all its problems gets in your way. Be confident in your ability and be realistic. Do not waste your time, energy, and money on the impossible and false unrealistic expectations. You know the difference between real and silly. You are a champion, you have confidence. You like yourself, you focus on your strengths, and these are all positive and good. However, never become arrogant, presumptuous, or vain. If you do, you will surely have a great and hard damaging fall, which will deliver you failure and despair. Never forget the true meaning of humility and try to live a humble life. I repeat often, humility is not thinking less of yourself but it is thinking of yourself less.

Carole receiving the love, prayers, encouragement, and praise of her mother gave Carole the perfect champion sentiment. Carole was taught to share daily her asset of humility. Like many mothers, Hazel was the leading influencer in Carole's maturity. She was Carole's number one enrichment in her life. Always building and establishing Carole's character. A mother's words and deeds go uninterrupted. They will forever remain popular and be desirous. A mother's love and care will never change and is needed in all aspects of a child's life. Nothing will or can replace the need for a good mother. A good mother is invaluable. I believe a mother's love is the closest we will get to the love of God. If you were like me and did not have the love of your mother, do not despair. It is up to us to make our life good and happy.

Hazel's tranquility made her a positive example for me and Carole to emulate. This was such a blessing because children want to express behavior like their mother's. Her unaggressive and gentle quietness was teaching us grit in reaching goals and solving problems while eliminating a lot of stress and anger. Hazel owned a pleasant demeanor. Even when some happenings in her life would have caused most anyone to become negative. She knew her attitude would create the emotion and mood of her family. Hazel was civil and not cantankerous. Her response to trouble was her fierce but silent show of resolve. Fortitude was one of her greatest strengths. Hazel's approach to life was traveling the road of self-discipline.

Carole and I have been blessed. She with a wonderful mother and father and me with a wonderful Mamaw, my great-grandfather, and Great-Aunt Lottie.

I hope there are caring people in your life that make you feel loved and wanted. I hope they are good examples for you. I hope you are being taught valuable lessons that will carry you through life.

We are never too old to learn. When needed, these learning experiences will surface. Take advantage of the opportunity you have been given. Do not disappoint the people who loved, cared, and sacrificed for you. Insist on living happy.

Hazel owns the definition of a mother's love. Even though she is not here with Carole anymore, her hugs and kisses will last a much long time, forever!

An amazing mother, one of the very best. Hazel's reward and crown in heaven will be "THE OSCAR."

It is said, "Mother is the name for God in the lips and hearts of her children."

The memory of people will come, and they will go in your life. But the memory of your mother, good or bad, will never leave you! A mother's eminence and importance far exceeds and is superior to all individuals. A good mother's love is never failing. She gave you life. She heard your first cry. A good mother will be your first love. If you were blessed with a good mother, thank God for this gift. If you do not have a good mother, thank God for holding you close and never abandoning you. His plan for you is a good life. A life of love, family, friends, and Jesus. He has made you strong.

Harold, Carole's Dad

Train up a child in the way he should go; and when he is old, he will not depart from it (Proverbs 22:6 KJV)

Harold was a kind and compassionate man. His heart and soul were good and wise. Always willing to give and do whatever it took to help someone in need. After studying and learning the situation, Harold would be quick to empathize. His empathy would show compassion, and he would offer his help. Sometimes I thought he was sensitive to a fault. Even so, he was emotionally strong. His strength was found in his words of guidance and his actions. He could imagine how he would feel and act if in their situation. He resonated with their pain. He felt their sorrow. He understood their emotions and could picture himself in their shoes. His good heart would always react with calm confident composure. Life's trials, when acting excitable and impetuous, would result in reckless and alarming decisions. His wisdom was being shown and taught to his daughter.

Harold was a quiet man. He did not have much to say. He always succeeded in saying all that was needed. He knew the right time to speak. He always timed his message when it was needed the most. Harold's voice was clear. With no unnecessary words. He never failed at letting his listener understand what he was communicating to them. His message some of the time was terse.

The lessons for Carole's future success and happiness were taught with love and rules. Harold did not make the rules appealing or pleasant. He did not make an excuse or make an apology to mollify Carole's feeling of being annoyed with his rules. He knew obedience would give assurance to Carole being able to care and protect herself when he could no longer be available.

Harold's daily thoughts and cares were about making sure his family, Hazel and Carole, were taken care of and provided for in every way. Like most men in Rosiclare, Harold worked for Alcoa in the mines. Carole learned from her dad the value of hard work and ambition. Like Hazel, Harold wanted for Carole a life of purpose, achievement, and gratification. He believed in being respectful to his coworkers at every level of Alcoa. Respect creates a just and equitable work environment for all employees. Respect promotes friendship, unity, and loyalty, thus making it easier to perform one's task; completing the work required.

Harold knew hard work fueled success. He always thought working for something brings greater pleasure and contentment than one gets because they are at the right place at the right time. Or better still, because they were lucky for a day.

Even though Harold was kind and sensitive to others' feelings, he was an involved dad. He expected instructions to be obeyed and common sense not to be a stranger. His rules were obeyed out of love, respect, and alarm at the unknown consequence of his choosing.

Harold wanted Carole to be an achiever. He knew lazy people would not grasp success and would never take advantage of an opportunity. Lazy people will always look for and find what they believe to be a legitimate excuse. They blame others for their inactive, idle, and unmotivated existence. They take no responsibility for contributing to a life with no objective. A life without purpose is a wasted life. It has no meaning and is a depressing and sad conclusion to what could have been very rewarding and happy.

Harold had no tolerance for laziness; therefore, he instilled in Carole that there is pride, integrity, and honor in hard work. It allows a person to respect themselves and allows them to be worthy of the respect of others. You gain knowledge, experience, and have the opportunity to promote friendship. You are now in charge of your fate. Harold prepared Carole with perseverance, discipline, and dedication. Understanding these character traits and inner qualities would give her possibilities for her goal in life. He believed in common sense risk. Risk that with hard work could be attainable. Harold grabbed onto, would hold firmly, never giving up on the hope of his daughter's future. Securing Carole's future was his most essential duty as a good dad. His aspirations for Carole seemed overarching at times. However, they were established with a dad's love promoting a strong desire in Carole's heart to strive for a life with purpose.

Like all good dads, Harold took his responsibility to Carole with sincerity. He provided her with the care she needed to be happy and to grow mentally, physically, and spiritually. He was a man who displayed his love for Carole through his advice, wisdom, discipline, and his encouragement. Harold gave thoughtful and consistent attention to the person she would become and to the future he wanted for her.

Harold wanted prosperity for Carole. His interpretation of prosperity for Carole was a rewarding career. A career that would give value, importance, and help to the disadvantaged, help to the depressed, the impoverished, the lonely, and the hopeless. Harold wanted her to have prosperity in health, friends, and happiness. Harold's faith, hard work, and goodwill meant prosperity. This was his definition of wealth.

His hope and dream for her was a career she loved, one she was unparalleled in, and one she would make beneficial contributions to mankind. He wanted her to remember the despairing and indigent with her all-encompassing wisdom and empathy. There are many troubles in every life. Chances of overcoming those troubles are greater when someone cares for and believes in you.

Carole found such a career. A job, position, and profession she excelled in far beyond reproach. She performed such a job and career for over thirty-five years. Harold's planning for Carole is now bringing to her the prosperity he had envisaged. She is a good friend to the forgotten and needy.

Harold told Carole that sometimes she would have a prestigious job, while other times her job might be unrewarding (it is called paying your dues), but none were beneath her. He taught her to respond with hard work and honesty. Whatever the job, she was to treat it with obligation and do the job with pride. Work gives you independence, dignity, usefulness, and income to sustain your needs. Many people have gone from humble beginnings to a flourishing career because they did their job and they did it right. Harold taught her to complete her obligation, hard or easy, and always do her best. A job well done will inspire, motivate, and empower others. Be unselfish and commit to grand success. This advice led to countless opportunities for Carole's career. All through our life, we will have many tasks we do not wish to do. But if it is our duty to complete and carry out, we will deliver. This duty to obligation will always be noticed and respected.

Carole's work was impeccable and accompanied with many accolades. But her most important reward was watching the people she helped improve their life. She is at her best when she is being of service to people who are experiencing hardship and misfortune. This attribute and inherent character belonging to Carole is a direct result of her wise mother and dad's teachings. It is the result of seeing her mother and dad's goodness and compassion for others in their time of need. These gracious and unselfish qualities in Hazel and Harold's nature were unveiled to Carole every day growing up. Just like Hazel buying Mamaw's cheap little pitcher so Mamaw could go to the doctor. The value of the little pitcher was nowhere near $20. Hazel and Harold were my family's first and only responders. Action solves all. Their life was all about benevolent helpful action. Another admirable characteristic belonging to Carole's parents. Harold would take me and Carole often to the Dairy Queen for our choice of ice cream. He always paid for mine. The only other time I got ice cream was my birthday. There was no room for ice cream in my family's $20 a week food budget. As a little girl, I did not know, and Harold and Hazel did not know of the love they would leave in my heart. Their love is still being felt today. Harold wanted for Carole a glorious future. I believe his hope and his faith rewarded him with this victory.

Harold communicated to Carole the value and potential a good education will provide. A good education will be the mainstay for a successful career. Harold was a wise man and always told Carole to choose her friends carefully. Have friends who share your faith, values, and judgment. He would tell her to choose friends who will boost and improve your belief and confidence in yourself. Friends with people you can always respect. Friends that will always respect you. The kind of respect you look for in friends does not come easy or quickly. It is earned from observing their words and their actions.

Her dad would train Carole to continue to seek wisdom. Wisdom is good sound prudent judgment. It is common sense. The wise are perceptive, and they observe. They have vision; however, they are shrewd.

Seeking wise counsel will strengthen your reasoning and decisiveness. The wise will find possibilities. They will finish with the best outcome. Harold was acquainting Carole with her moral fiber. To build her backbone and be tough as steel when necessary. Conditioning her to be independent and not be influenced by others. He wanted Carole to rely on wisdom, good conscience, and he wanted her to hear her heart speak. He wanted her decisions to be made with self-control. Not to wait but to dig in and finish the task. He taught her how to survive and to thrive when problems came her direction.

Harold is no longer here. He passed away knowing the job he was given was a success. That job was just being Carole's dad. An unassuming man who did not need to feel important. He did not need praise or applaud of approval. Harold was a common man. A man who kept his promise and kept his word. A good dad leaving Carole a legacy of love, devotion, and counsel.

Harold was an educator, enforcer, and an encourager.

Harold had the bark of the wise!

Harold, Hazel, and Carole. My always faithful only other family.

Me and Hazel

13

Carole, My Irreplaceable Friend

As each has received a gift, use it to serve one another, as good stewards of God's varied grace. (1 Peter 4:10 ESV)

Family is not always blood. It is people in your life who want to be around you; people who accept you as you are, will do anything to make you smile, and will be there for you in the happy and sad. This is my best friend Carole. Carole, her mother and dad moved next door to me, Mamaw, Pa, and Aunt Lottie when Carole was not even one year old. I was twenty-six months of age. We were probably friends and playing together before Carole could walk. Our houses were in close proximity. They were next door to each other.

Carole was an only child, and I was an only child. We filled each other's days having fun, playing games, making dreams, and forming a lasting friendship that was facilitated, guarded, protected, and kept by God. We were together every day while growing up in Rosiclare. Carole's mother and dad and my Mamaw's core values, beliefs, and principles were equivalent. Their parenting skill and parenting method they practiced when interacting with and raising a child were compatible. They were a duplicate of each other regarding mine and Carole's treatment and instruction we received throughout our childhood. Carole and I know they all three were superstars. They showed us every day their love was unconditional. I always say, "My Mamaw raised me and Carole, and Hazel, Carole's mother, raised Carole and me."

They brought us to church faithfully. To them going to church was like going to school. It was required, expected, and obligatory. Going to church was never optional or voluntary. We went to the same little church in Rosiclare until I was about twelve years old, and Carole was about ten years! We sang in church often. Every Sunday night this elderly farmer wearing his bib overalls would request Carole and me to sing. We always had a song ready and always granted to this fine old gentleman his request. I will never forget those Christian hymns.

Our church had a pastor that was a good man. However, he was a poor preacher. Of course, Rosiclare did not always have seminary educated pastors. This preacher had very little if any qualification of schooling providing education or training in theology. His sermons were all the same. Always advising the congregation all alcohol should be thrown in the river. Brother H made many blunders. He was lacking in all requirement.

Carole and I were impish and slightly naughty little girls. We would giggle at his many noticeable and careless debacles and gaffes. We always were required to sit close to Mamaw and Hazel so they could see we were behaving. Somehow they never learned of our disrespect for Brother H. Good thing for us they never knew. They demanded total obedience of us in church. Carole and I tried to deliver on their absolute authority of good conduct in church service. Every Sunday we struggled to control our annoyance and boredom. Brother H's pulpit delivery and sermon provided on too many occasions humor and amusing entertainment for me and Carole. The church must have recognized this too. They did not continue with him as pastor very long.

Now Carole and I live on a road that had only four houses. Her house was the last, and my house was next to the last. When we were little, we always had a lemonade stand on the road in front of my house. We never sold one glass of lemonade. But that did not stop us. Every Summer until we got to be about nine and eleven years old, we had that lemonade stand. Always in the same place and never made a sale.

Hazel and Mamaw were so protective of us. We were trick-or-treating on Halloween before anyone. We were getting home about the time everyone else was going out. Rosiclare had a theater. We went to the movie every Sunday after church. Back then it cost 25¢ to see the movie. We rode our bicycles all over Rosiclare.

The churches had rummage sales. I would buy the high heels and hats. Carole would buy the purses and dresses. We played house a lot, we also formed a club. We charged the neighborhood one cent to be a member of our club. We also did not make money at that endeavor. No members but me and Carole. We had fun and considered our club a success.

The Barbie doll was introduced to Rosiclare March 1959. We both got one. I think we played dolls longer than anybody.

We played in the snow. We lived behind the grade school. The schoolyard was one big hill. We had so much fun sleigh riding on that hill in the Illinois snow.

We also got to go roller skating. Carole's dad would take us. Rosiclare had a nice roller rink. Carole learned to be good on skates. I never did. I was always scared and a bit clumsy too.

Carole got the measles, and I got the mumps. As soon as we got over them, Carole had the mumps, and I got the measles. We played together from morning till late evening in the summer. We could always be found in the company of each other.

We had our share of fights when we were young. I think even today we are each wearing a scar we donated to each other when fighting. The area between mine and Carole's house was gravel. Unfortunately, that is where we did most of our fighting.

I disliked mustard. Carole had a sandwich, and I asked if it had mustard. She said no! Well, it did! I took a bite, and that started a big battle, began a war.

We each had a dog. They were brothers, and we named them Rover and Dover. We took our dogs on picnics often. The picnic area was always the schoolyard in front of our houses. We made our picnic lunch. Our lunch was always identical. We made the same picnic lunch every time. Lunch was butter and sugar sandwiches. We would take a bite, and then we would give Rover and Dover a bite. Our dogs loved the sandwich. It is a wonder and surprise we did not get sick from eating after our dogs.

Carole and I remain close today with more than seventy years of friendship behind us. We text and talk weekly, even though I am in South Carolina and she in Illinois. We manage to see each other every couple of years.

In all our years of friendship, Carole has never let me down. No one could ask for a better friend. I do not have another person outside my immediate family who even comes close to Carole's many distinctive attributes and characteristics describing our friendship. I am so blessed to have her in my life.

I can trust Carole with anything. My secrets are safe with Carole. Maybe because of the abandonment issue, I have never had confidence in myself. Carole always assured me and had faith in my ability to achieve my goals and dreams. She always knew the right thing to say, the right action to take in helping me through my insecurities and feelings of being inconsequential.

I was and I am always assured of Carole's friendship. She allows me to let my guard down and express myself more openly and honestly. I do not have to pretend around Carole. She knows my fears, deepest desires, strengths, and weaknesses. I do not let my guard down with many people. I have built a wall around myself thinking it will keep me from being hurt and disappointed. I realize I need to let my guard down so others will know who I really am. It has always been hard for fear of being disliked. I was betrayed by my parents, and in some ways, that painful realization still causes me agony.

I am afraid of looking vulnerable and exposed. Trust is an issue for me. I trust my best girlfriend, Carole, wholeheartedly and without hesitation. I never need to defend myself with Carole. She does not criticize, and she is nonjudgmental. She genuinely accepts me for who I am. And she respects my feelings. Carole believes in constructive prudent advice because she wants to see me and others succeed. You cannot be in the company of Carole without recognizing the Holy Spirit to be in reach. Carole's love for Jesus is evident by the example of her life. She is always focused and deeply invested in being a witness for her Savior, Jesus Christ. Carole lives it and walks it like she talks it! She is genuine in her relationship with God. She is unmistakably genuine in her relationship with all others. Carole keeps her word and will always show sensibly.

She is consistent and stable. Carole can be depended on, regardless of my need, and she will expect nothing in return. The parenting Carole received gave her the gift to be capable of sending strong messages. Messages that make an individual think, plan, and prepare. Messages of faith, hope, and wisdom which will carry a strong and lasting positive effect on the lives of others. I may not like what I hear, but I know it is said with the best of intentions.

Carole and I know that we are a priority to each other. We respect one another and can spend time together just being ourselves, displaying our vulnerability, our goofy side, and our weirdness. She is there to comfort, support, laugh, cry, congratulate, or just listen. Our friendship has endured many years and separated by many miles; however, I believe our friendship grows stronger with every passing year. We share gifts, we give praise, we exchange compliments, and we promise all our devotion to this lasting friendship often and spontaneously.

I thank God for all the wonderful people he has put in my life. They all have been a blessing. Everything God does for you is part of his plan. And when finished, God's plan for you will have satisfied all the necessary requirements and qualities for a life lived with purpose, a life of contribution, and not a life of taking, receiving, conspiring, and nonearning. The life of freeloader, the individual who takes and never gives, will give you no self-respect, no ambition, will waste your talent, and deliver you to defeat. You are his child, and he loves you. He will favor you and never leave you. Nothing can ever separate you from his love. Hold your head high and "look what God WILL DO."

God endowed and gifted Carole with the talent to genuinely want to help those less fortunate. He allowed her the ability to acquire the skill through hours and years of education. Her devoted time, effort, and tenacity have proven to bring perfection to this God-given talent. This was God calling to Carole; it was part of his plan for her. She has always given of her time and her possessions to those in need. She has been able to enhance the well-being of so many. She is good at helping with very basic needs and also good at helping those with difficult complex issues and unpredicted circumstances. She has always been attentive, concerned and touched by the sorrows troubling the oppressed and the poor. It is without fail her plan to get them to a place in life where their mental and physical health greatly improves. To try to show them how to achieve comfort and contentment. And to witness they can attain the happiness and peace they long for and desire through their relationship with Jesus Christ. Carole has been very successful in achieving her goals, dreams, and passion. They are bettering, rehabilitating, and bolstering up the personality, character, and lives of the disadvantaged, underprivileged, helpless, and abused.

Carole has a caring and compassionate heart. Carole feels others' pain. She knows what is needed to alleviate and mitigate their agony and distress. Carole takes action immediately using her knowledge, professionalism, and skillfulness. The favorable result and success to all we aspire to, our ambitions, our endeavors present and future are work, tenacity, and faith. It is, NEVER QUIT—NEVER GIVE UP.

Carole was determined in the plan God had for her life. She worked and put her way through school, earning a master's degree in social work. She worked with special needs in the school system, serving as a counselor and advocate for the children and their parents. Carole worked in healthcare for thirty-nine years at the Hardin County Hospital in Rosiclare. There she assisted patients and families to deal and cope with health issues. She arranged for community services when they would go home. Carole worked in the emergency room handling crisis intervention for drug addictions, suicidal patients, victims of abuse, etc.

The last seven years, Carole provided counseling and was the director of a Behavioral Health program at Hardin County General Hospital. She conducted group therapy three days a week, three sessions a day. After thirty-nine years, she decided it was time to retire and enjoy doing things with her amazing husband, Roger. Carole and Roger love to travel, and they love fishing. They both love serving the Lord and work tirelessly in their church. And of course, Carole is still helping others. She is and always will be available to assist anyone who needs help. Her ability and her gift to comfort, listen, and support have benefited many.

Having Carole in your life in any terms of capacity will create for you an abundance of blessings. Carole does good to everyone. When in the company of Carole, she initiates and creates an atmosphere of welcoming. She sets the tone for orderly conduct. She invites everyone to share in her goodness.

Carole will not allow you to take advantage of her good nature. Her personality is strong. It is assertive, focused, and determined to stay true to her values. She has much charisma; however, she will not back down. She will not let you compromise her fearlessness, her total security, and her clear vision of the situation. She holds good character and her winning personality should never be underestimated. Carole's conviction and commitment to her closely held beliefs, principles, and opinions guarantee her a win every time. Carole will always be polite. She has a refined and well-spoken manner. Without exception, she will be better prepared for the challenge than all others. She goes for the win!

Carole is a woman of purpose and power. She has her mother's realistic optimism. Optimistic people are self-motivated. They know uncomfortable situations emerge in every life. But the optimist will immediately search for ways to mend and repair. They see the problem to have a positive and gratifying result. The optimistic mental attitude sees only the good and never the negative. They do not ignore life problems. They just observe and study them through stronger eyeglasses and lenses than the pessimist and the doubter. The optimist does not pretend. They do not choose to wait on others to make life good. They use their energy, they use their strong never-give-up willpower, they determine a realistic solution, and they go to work with action. A sure way to get good results is to attend to them yourself.

We are all pure gold inside. We are all important. Our skills and talents may not yet be developed. Have a goal, realize a dream, keep a promise, work hard, be persistent despite the obstacles that will try your will. Carole can most assuredly share this process in life because she lived it. Her experience reaching her dream and putting into service her calling did not come easy or quickly. Carole did not quit or give up. She knew God works on his time clock and not hers.

There have been many times Carole has used her heart and her profession to coach me to let go of many issues caused by my abandonment. The most valued was Carole always showed me she loved me and thought of me as her sister, and she would never abandon me. She always shared good advice. She gave common sense taught by Hazel and Harold. A friend like Carole happens very few times in a person's life. It is much easier for most people to be preoccupied with oneself. Easy to be selfish, forgetting to show concern, consideration, and help to their friend in need. The quality of my friendship with Carole has never been nor will it ever be matched by anyone. All my life I have heard it said that an old friend is the best friend. Carole and I hold dear, respect, cherish, and we always connect back to our deeply held values, principles, and ethics. These were all baked into our souls with devotion, nurturing, teaching, training, and love. All this awarded us by the wonderful people who were always in attendance while we were growing up. They also instilled in us to stay motivated. To have a driving force within us that will never be stopped. Think of your goals with passion and imagination. Motivation is your engine. Money is not always success. Be proud of making life more important than it.

I understand there cannot help but be obstacles for me caused by my mother and dad. I remember but I do not make their abandonment of me as an infant the focal point in my life. With the love, constancy, and loyalty of the wonderful people I write about, I have survived. They all helped this innocent and forgotten little girl overcome the seriousness and damage caused her. They would help mend my lack of self-worth and confidence. They realized if not corrected this would give sobering limitations to my future.

Do not cling to your past. It will pull you down like an anchor. It will cloud your mind with pain, hurt, and much negatives. Think about all the blessings in your life. Keep your attainable realistic dreams alive. Make good progress in your life advancing a purpose-filled future. Move forward with your plan remembering my grandmother's core values. I have lived many times my grandmother's words, "You are stronger than you think. NEVER QUIT—NEVER GIVE UP."

When life has taken an unfavorable lead and direction as it often will, stay optimistic. There is tomorrow, and faith is working and planning good things. Pause and go forward with good actions. Engaging in bad behavior, performing bad conduct, will deliver you punishment. Live in faith, let God lead your days, and look at what God WILL DO!

The value of Carole in my life is beyond measure. We have made mud pies together, started our business partnership with the lemonade stand, played many games together, talked about boys, and shared our hopes and dreams. I give thanks for the laughter, the loyalty, the listening, the understanding, the compassion, the acceptance, the trust, and the prayers we have shared.

Carole is the kind of person and friend who is predictable. She always gives consolation in times of worry, concern, or grief. She is there to love, praise, serve, encourage, and provide assistance.

Carole is a courageous believer. She is not afraid to express opposition. She is not afraid of the unknown. It is called having faith and knowing God is in control.

Carole worked very hard putting herself through college. Carole's parents, like most families in Rosiclare, did not have the money to pay for her education. But what they did do was give her a good chance at a purposeful life. Carole was determined. She knew what she wanted in life was to give help to the less fortunate. She excelled at her career. She did not quit on her passion and her dream even though there were many times she struggled with what appeared to be impossible. Many times Carole became disheartened in completing her education, but she always kept clarity. She was steadfast. She stayed the course to the end. She achieved her goal. She made her parents proud, for she chose a career they admired, acclaimed, and valued.

Carole completed her education and found a rewarding career. She did all this by utilizing the teachings of Hazel and Harold. She won and earned the respect and admiration of her superiors, her peers, her subordinates, and all the many people she helped. Carole is her parents' accomplishment. Her parents taught Carole to get a good education. They taught her to be an independent, contributing, forgiving, woman. They demonstrated to her that people are influenced by acts of kindness. They trained Carole to always keep learning. They acquainted her to be a doer and to take action. They taught her to share the good things in her life. They instilled in her the importance of giving back to and contributing to her community. Carole's parents told her to smile often. The power of a smile can bring hope, peace, improve attitudes, and bring comfort to the troubled. The actions and examples Carole witnessed daily of her parents gave her common sense and wisdom. Common sense and wisdom allow a person to hear, think rationally, make choices to help your future, omit your emotions when making a decision, and keep a person living in reality. Without common sense and wisdom, you can be assured life will be reckless, impulsive, chaotic, arbitrary, and confused.

True friends are hard to find. We need to let them know how much they mean to us. We need to tell them how much they have enhanced the quality of our life. How they have improved all areas of our life, such as our physical, mental, and spiritual health. We are never alone if we have a good friend. They will always be there to lift us up when we are down.

Carole has been a paragon, the perfect example to so many people, especially to those who need a friend, confident, or just someone who shows they care. Carole is worthy of being declared a model person. She is an individual to be copied, to be imitated, and to strive for her equal. She has so many admirable qualities to her character. Her entire life has been serving as a guide and teacher. She inspires and demonstrates to children and adults how to live with optimism, hope, determination, forgiveness, and honesty. Carole's constitution is evident and on display, always behaving in a way that shows obedience to her mother and dad's rules and her deep desire to please and not disappoint the two people who loved her unconditionally. Two people known as Hazel and Harold. The evidence of the life Carole lives gives notice and recognition to the counsel and instruction of her parents.

Growing up in Rosiclare, Carole was my playmate and friend. Her parents blessed me always with kindness in their words and actions.

The 1950s and 1960s were a good time in America to be a child. Carole and I had people in our lives who were determined to make our lives better than theirs. The things they gave us that still today we remember and use throughout our life were all free of the cost of money. They have been of more value to us than anything money could have bought. Mamaw, Hazel, and Harold had no wealth, but they knew the definition of rich.

Carole and her mother share in the right of owning the word optimism. They always saw the positive outcome to every negative situation. They both will go to work immediately, pouring all their energy, talent, confidence, and toil in guaranteeing their desired result.

Of course, we do not receive 100 percent of the time our wants and wishes. But with Carole and her mother's never-defeatist attitude, they are able to stay focused on their goal. The power of a winning attitude will produce success and victory many times over.

Carole was put in my life for a reason. She was meant for His plan. Carole's friendship to me is authentic and sincere. It is flawless. For over seventy years, her friendship to me has gone unbroken.

117

Me, Carole, and my dog Dover with my house in the background.

Me and Carole. Best friends still today.

Me and Carole at my house.

Me and Carole. Best friends for more than 75 years.

Me and my cherished friend, Carole.

14

Gary—My Husband, My Prince Charming

People say a lot of the time a girl will love and marry a man who reminds her of her dad. Great-grandfather, Pa, was the only dad figure I ever knew. He and Uncle Ben were the only men I ever loved prior to Gary. I loved Pa the most and the longest because he loved me from the time I was twenty-one months old until he passed away. I was twenty-one years in age when Pa ceased living. I followed through on the reality many girls marry men calling to mind the memory of their dad. This feeling of nostalgia for me brought back many beautiful hints of days spent with Pa. Days past and gone but always remembered with love and gratitude.

Gary had many of the same qualities and characteristics as Pa. They both had personality traits which caused people to like, respect, and want to be in their company of friends. Both were friendly, patient, reliable, helpful, loyal, and very slow to anger. Gary and Pa were the kindest men I have ever known.

I knew the kind of person and husband I would be getting with Gary. In fifty years of marriage, he never let me down. He made my life overflowing with happiness. He brought to fruition my expectations and dreams of the man I would one day want to marry. There were no surprises with Gary. He was a devoted husband and father. God knew the kind of husband I would need. He gave me Gary. God's decision and his timing were perfect.

When I was little, Cinderella was my favorite fairy tale. I remember being in kindergarten when the Rosiclare senior class gave their acting debut to the elementary school children. They performed the story of Cinderella. I remember sitting on the floor of the high school gymnasium directly in front of the stage. I was five years old, and I loved the play. To this day, the story of Cinderella is still my favorite fairy tale. I still love going to see the live performances of a theatrical play. The beauty and the love of Cinderella and Prince Charming remain everlasting in my memory.

As a grown woman, when I think of the lasting impression of the fairy tale, Cinderella, I know of God's presence in my young life that day. He was assuring me his plan for my life would consist of a Prince Charming. In my life so many times, I accept and I take to heart the words of my wise grandmother. She always told me people who do not dream never have a dream come true. I dreamed of a Prince Charming.

I know fairy tales are children's stories of questionable events. These events are probably never going to happen. However, sometimes in our life we may have experiences that remind us of a fairy tale. I lived such an experience I will share with you.

All fairy tales begin with, "Once upon a time" or "A long, long time ago." They tell their listener or their reader "the characters lived happily ever after." The fairy tale of Cinderella performed by Rosiclare High School seniors that day conveyed to those young and impressionable elementary school children how they should treat others. The fairy tale revealed to them being kind, having patience, and courage rendered rewards. And the greatest of these rewards was love.

My husband, Gary, proved to be my Prince Charming. Just like the fairy tale, Gary was put in my life coming to the rescue of a young girl in distress. He was kind, brave, generous, compassionate, supportive, and would be my sweetheart for more than fifty years. Gary always showed good manners, always courteous. He was a charmer and very charismatic. People wanted to be in his presence. He had beautiful bright blue eyes that always twinkled. When you looked into Gary's twinkling eyes, you saw happy, optimism, and kindness. His eyes spoke to you with sincerity, confidence, humor, hope, friendship, and wisdom.

When I met Gary, I thought he was the most handsome man I had ever seen. Thick blonde curly hair and big bright blue eyes. He was complementary, considerate, courteous, pleasant, and he made a shy and naive young girl feel comfortable, safe, and at ease.

I decided that day Gary would be my husband. He did not know he would marry me, but I knew I would marry him. I was patient and did not show annoyance or frustration when waiting for him to propose marriage. Gary was not easy for me to catch. I loved this man and I would NEVER QUIT—NEVER GIVE UP. I was living the magic of my favorite fairy tale. God's plan for me was Gary.

I was living in Jacksonville, Illinois. I went to Jacksonville a few days after my high school graduation in June 1965. I found employment working as a secretary. I was very shy in those days. I had never been away from my grandmother and Rosiclare. The only people I had any kind of relationship with are the people I talk about in this book. I had no friends from my school years. I had my next-door best friend Carole. There were a couple of girls who lived close to me, and we would be good acquaintances and neighbors. However, I would not refer to them as friends. I was not good at making friends in those days, and today it is still very hard for me to make friends. I had lived a sheltered life, and I had lived to some degree a lonely life. In Jacksonville, I worked at a job that only paid $100 per week. That was the common income pay scale for secretarial jobs in 1965.

Now on my own and not eighteen years old for a couple of months. I had no family, no friends, and no money. However, just like the fairy tale, God assigned to me my fairy godmother, my guardian angel. This guardian angel would protect me from danger and give me the courage to stay true to my core values taught to me by my grandmother. My guardian angel sent by God would do for me what Cinderella's fairy godmother did for her. This angel would lead a path for me to follow. A path to keep my feet standing firm on the ground making sensible decisions. God had a plan for my life and he would not allow his plan to fail.

"Once upon a time," "A long time ago," a charming, young, handsome, kind prince named Gary asked me for a date, mine and Gary's first date was August 10, 1965. I was seventeen years old, and my eighteenth birthday was coming soon, August 27. I was renting a room in a big house that mirrored the resemblance of a castle. The couple who lived at and owned the house rented the five bedrooms upstairs to single girls. They hung a sign on the front door that read, "The Castle." I have given attention before to God's amazing and amusing sense of humor. For my eighteenth birthday, Gary sent me one dozen red roses, and Gary's card read, "Happy birthday to the princess in the castle." I kept the card. Beginning with five-year-old kindergarten and continuing, I had dreamed and wished for my favorite fairy tale and love story to somehow find its way to my lonely and insecure life. God arranged it all. He assured me that day Gary was his choice for my prince charming.

We dated until Gary left for the US Navy on Thanksgiving Day 1965. We wrote each other often and we talked on the phone frequently. We spent time together when he came home on leave from his service to our country. My husband was a very intelligent man with good strong hard-working ethics. Gary spent seven years in the Nuclear Navy. He would spend four of those years in school for the Navy receiving a nuclear education. The remaining three years would be spent active duty assigned to a fleet ballistic missile nuclear submarine. The navy gave Gary the assignment of nuclear reactor operator. Not everyone can get qualified for this position. Being the submarine nuclear reactor operator required the individual to be of high intelligence and quick, good mental capacity and would need to think before they spoke or acted. Gary was always good at controlling and keeping command of his emotions. He was always a very patient man. He could easily adapt to change, and he was self-motivating. Gary had the mental, emotional, and physical ability to solve problems of any nature without the help of anyone except Jesus. He was compassionate and caring. Gary was curious about everything, and he never stopped reading, studying, and learning. He was observant and never missed a thing. Gary could do several things at the same time; he would read, watch television, and have a coherent conversation with me. All this done at the same time. He was not a worrier. He took care of the things in life that were within his control. The rest he would accept and adjust accordingly. Gary had a tremendous vocabulary. This was achieved by his passion to keep learning, educating, accomplishing, and being proficient at any and all of his life's endeavors.

Gary was loyal, dependable, tenacious, service-driven, cordial, humble, and wise. He could follow directions. Gary was obedient, understanding the rules and regulations requirements. He had all the necessary attributes and qualities in his character securing him the reputation of being an exemplary person. This exemplary person reputation applied to both Gary's professional life and his personal life. He was kind, helpful, and generous to everyone. Jesus walked with my husband every day of his life sharing with Gary his kindness, mercy, goodness, and love. And Jesus would instruct Gary to share the gifts and blessings given to him with others. And Gary obeyed Jesus's directive every day of his life. Almost everyone I knew, sooner or later, would tell me I was very fortunate, or very blessed, or favored, or just lucky to have Gary as my husband. I knew I was all of the above. God had delivered on my dream of prince charming. My life was meant to be shared with Gary. God will make no mistakes in the plan he has for your life.

We were married on January 26, 1969, in Jacksonville. We were married in mine and Gary's church. It was also the church of his family. He was stationed in Charleston, South Carolina. Just married and filled with hope for a long, happy life together.

Gary and I have two daughters. Our oldest daughter, Stephanie, was born on January 11, 1970. Our second daughter, Stacy, was born on February 20, 1971. We all live in the same town and see each other often. Both girls are such a blessing. They never gave us worry or caused problems. Both girls married godly men whom Gary and I love and highly approve. We are blessed with 3 wonderful grandchildren.

Gary completed his duty and obligation to the US Navy and was honorably discharged in October 1972. All the education and experience he received in the Navy assured him a great career with Duke Energy Company. Duke Energy is a very large, reputable, and leader in nuclear power in the Carolinas. They provide power to many. Duke has three nuclear plants, of which Gary was employed for forty-three years. Gary's career span with Duke Energy gave him gratification and many years of continued learning, education, and experience. He enjoyed and appreciated the opportunity to be associated with Duke. Gary excelled at his job. He was superior and successful in his achievements. Duke recognized this and rewarded Gary several times, showing their respect and appreciation of him.

While at Duke Energy, Gary was presented with the James B. Duke award. This award was given to Gary in 2010. The award recognizes employees for the most exceptional, significant achievements supporting the company's goals, values, and principles. The recipients of this award are nominated and selected by their peers. Gary was given this award for saving the life of a coworker. Gary gave a quick assessment of the severity of the employee's injury. His decisions that day proved to be life-saving actions at the most critical time. Gary's calm and decisive handling of a serious situation ensured a positive ending to what could have been a tragedy. Most everything

I wrote regarding Gary's award can be found in the exact wording of the 2010 James B. Duke Awards, honoring 2009 achievements. We have Duke's written award, with the wording I gave you, framed and on a wall in our home. Gary's training in the Nuclear Navy and his training at Duke Energy was used that day. Gary was always able to manage his emotions and rely on his training. He was prepared for this bad experience because of all the on-the-job teaching, instruction, and education he received in the US Navy and Duke Energy.

Gary was very active in the American Legion. He was the South Carolina State Commander of the American Legion in 2012. Everyone knows the American Legion is a nonprofit organization whose members are US veterans. This organization is committed to so many programs that provide for veterans and their families. One of the many blessings, honors, and memories for Gary was being asked to lay the wreath at the tomb of the unknown soldier on Veterans Day 2012. He cherished this privilege and honor. It was an emotional and heartwarming experience for Gary. These sentiments indicated his love for his country. They also expressed the value and appreciation Gary placed on our country's armed veterans who served and paid the ultimate sacrifice with their life. This was a very humbling experience for Gary. We owe a debt to these American heroes we will never be able to pay. Their memory and sacrifice stand on the shoulders of the patriot.

Gary thought everyone was important. He was extremely intelligent, but he was humble. He was always interested in learning more and trying new things. He was always in pursuit, chasing his vision for the future. He never put limits on what he could do or the contributions he could offer. Gary kept busy. He had an active life, and his life did not go unnoticed. Gary was nonconfrontational. He would not engage in conversation crowded with anger. He was a good communicator and a good listener. He did not worry; however, he would be concerned. He thought worry was a waste of time. He could always take on challenges with patience. He was resilient and determined. He embraced life and took and put to use every opportunity. But Gary never took more than he gave. He was open to new ideas, but he would question your judgment. He questioned everything, gathering facts before coming to a conclusion. He worked well under pressure and would not show signs of being nervous, having doubt, or being irritated. His patience was his silent hope and promise of having a good ending to the situation. Gary was diligent and gave persevering attention to everything in doing his job. Getting the job done right was important to him and this was always his priority.

Being abandoned as an infant, I brought with me to the marriage insecurities by the many. I never talked to Gary about my childhood. But, of course, he knew Mamaw raised me. I never talked to or discussed with anyone being abandoned. I never discussed the problems and issues caused by my parents until I was past sixty years old. Gary, Mamaw, Pa, Aunt Lottie, Carole, and her parents knew of the sadness and hurt but they never mentioned anything. They all tried in every way they could to assure me of their love.

I never had to doubt Gary's love, devotion, and support. He was my friend, confidant, sweetheart, and husband for over fifty years. He gave me purpose, confidence, and a good life. Gary was all this broken young girl from Rosiclare would need to carry out the plan God had designed for her life. Unlike my parents, I was assured of Gary's love. I knew he would never abandon me. I have loved Gary since before my eighteenth birthday. I still love him today and always. There is rarely a day that goes by that I do not thank God for the perfect man he put in my life. A man who would help me accomplish my dreams and goals. Gary would strengthen me always. Gary was free with and gave often affection, compliments, tenderness, and endearments all through our married life.

Gary was a man who stayed busy. He occupied his time being productive. He planned his objectives; he was self-motivated and committed to finishing his specific plan. He was always searching for long-term gains. Gary never allowed his emotions to cloud or lead his mind. He was the best at self-control. He set boundaries with his time both personally and professionally. He was his own designer-architect when it came to his judgment, decision-making, and choices for his life. He would take into careful consideration wise advice as needed.

Gary gave me his extraordinary love. Every insecurity I dealt with as a result of being abandoned by my mother and dad, Gary understood. He never grew tired of loving me. He was never reluctant and always determined to help me overcome all the problems of abandonment. A person never forgets. Sometimes those old hurts and wounds still get in my way. However, with Gary at my side for over fifty years, I was able to lock them away in my mind, locked away far enough.

Gary and I both worked hard at our professions and our jobs. We liked to travel, going to the mountains and beach often. We did travel abroad on three different occasions. We enjoyed our travel outside the country, absorbing the culture, landscape, and history of the places we visited. We both were captivated by the beautiful architecture. We were fascinated with the cuisine. It was amazing how the same foods we prepare in America, when cooked based on another country's tradition, are sometimes only slightly identifiable. We found the people to be charming. Sometimes we made a couple of acquaintances from America. We always enjoyed these visits, touring as much of the country as possible. We made many lasting and beautiful memories. And of course, there were always trips to Illinois to visit family and friends.

Gary knew God had another job for him. It would be his most important job. It would be the job he loved and treasured the most. This job would give Gary two amazing prizes. This job would require him to stay interested, require him to set expectations for himself and his two prizes, he would be required to invest time, and offer the best opportunity possible. He would be required to deliver toughness, and he would be required to not fail but to be a success. This big job would never end and would never be completed. There would be no money given and no money earned with this forever job. Given all this, the job had a paramount title that was superior to all others. The title of the job Gary had been given was, "DAD!"

Mine and Gary's girls are thirteen months apart. They are the greatest joy of our life. Gary's love for the girls was bountiful. Gary realized strong bonds with his daughters would be accomplished by giving them his time. He was always available for talk, support, and encouragement. He was always ready to help with school homework and projects. It was determined when they were small children college was in their future. Gary had a way of discussing the importance of education that made the girls want to go to college. Together they built their strong loving relationship. A relationship built on family traditions. Those family traditions grounded thoroughly into their character by their dad are being passed down to Gary's grandchildren. We always ate dinner as a family. Much good family time was spent at the dinner table. One of the girls' fondest memories of their dad when they were little was going to the service station with him. This always meant Coca-Cola, M&M's candy, and comic books. The girls loved and were proud of their dad and did not want to disrespect or disappoint him. They were good children, and they never gave us trouble. Gary made sure both girls knew where his friendship ended. And he made sure they knew where his parental love, guidance, and accountability commenced. The girls knew their dad loved them, but they knew he would hold them accountable. A good earthly dad will correct his children. Gary knew no discipline given Stephanie and Stacy when needed would bring joy to the girls. He knew no discipline when children have disobeyed would prove to be troublesome in their future. A view of authority and punishment is hard on the parent. It is necessary for the child's future behavior. It teaches them to make better decisions in all areas of their life. It teaches them to learn from their mistakes. Good discipline for children secures rewards.

Gary taught the girls good work ethics. When they turned sixteen years old, they both got part-time jobs during the school year. In the summer, the job became full-time. Both girls worked all through high school and college. Today, they are both independent. They both made good choices in their husbands. Like their dad, the girls glorify God. They are both faithful to their church. Gary has a grandson named after him. He looks like and has many of the attributes and mannerisms of his granddaddy. Gary asked God to guide his daughters' lives, keeping them in step with his son, Jesus. When you marry, make sure that person is a practicing Christian. You never want one partner to walk in light and the other to walk in darkness. That will not make a Christian marriage or a Christian home.

The girls knew their dad's love for them was unconditional and was shown to be of great quantity. They knew nothing nor anyone would ever damage or destroy his devotion and his everlasting love and allegiance to them. Gary held his daughters close to his heart and mind. He would always be prepared to take his responsibility. Gary would be a dedicated dad. Gary understood the meaning of dad. He understood the joy. He understood his leadership was not only his obligation but it was essential.

God blessed Gary with these two prizes, Stephanie and Stacy. Gary accepted these two blessings with willingness to seek out and ask for God's guidance and direction. The job was big and at times it would require much effort, understanding, talent, skill, etc. It was a demanding and complicated job that Gary loved. He accomplished his biggest job well, enriching the quality of his children's lives.

Everything Gary and I worked for was to build a future for our children. We knew there would be days when success would not happen. But we kept working hard, we took action, made reachable goals, prudent good judgment, and we were persistent. We knew we would encounter storms. Remember life has many storms, but storms, obstacles, and difficulties make us stronger. We believed in our potential and we had hope.

Remember you are stronger and more capable than you think. Everyone has a talent, a gift, a passion, ability, a distinctive quality, to be continuously and regularly worked by you, to come to fruition. Everyone needs a purpose in life. Hard work and tenacity along with wisdom are needed to attain your goals. Some of the most successful people have failed several times. You will not be successful, you will not have a purposeful life, you will not be living your passions, goals, and values if you stop trying.

Remember what my grandmother drilled into my consciousness: "NEVER QUIT—NEVER GIVE UP." Maintain a strong willpower. Your willpower is like a big canyon filled with confidence, purpose, goals, ambition, self-discipline, and motivation. Willpower is your inner strength, your moral fiber, and it defines the substance of which you are made. You do not inherit willpower. It is you developing your mindset with a good attitude revealing work and effort. Give service to others. Show no temper, no anger, be determined, be prepared, be willing, and be committed to achieving. Take nothing for granted. Live in the future. Let go of the past. Your parents' dereliction of duty and shameful abandonment of you will not govern and determine your life. You alone will decide to be happy. Incorrigible bad parents won the battle when you were little and needed them. Even as a child and certainly now, you observed, you learned, and you enriched yourself, making friends and keeping company with honest good people. Character of these individuals resonated with you and inspired you to live a life of goodwill and purpose. You learned from them not everyone will treat you mercilessly and acrimoniously as did your parents. Don't allow the mistakes of your absent parents to define you. Create connections with people you respect. Like yourself. Live a life you can be proud of—know you are equally important as anyone. HOLD YOUR HEAD HIGH!

Gary always listened and heard what was being said. He evaluated everything he heard. His mind was always working. The girls knew Gary loved them with all his heart and soul. He showed them all his hope for achieving, showed them all his effort in teaching a good attitude. Showed them the importance of giving honor to everyone by being kind and pleasant in words and actions. He taught them to be thankful for their many blessings. The girls were the recipient of most of Gary's prayers. He gave his children all his strength, courage, and his love for life and learning. He brought to their attention and made them aware of humility. His girls were watching. Their dad's many and varied good deeds done his entire life for the betterment of others. Gary never grew tired or became discouraged in helping people and accommodating their needs. He would find every day an opportunity to offer goodness, kindness, and unselfishness.

Every family and life has struggles and challenges. Our family was no different from all others. But Gary was always there to fix the concern. He was the faithful leader in our home. Gary trusted God. Gary had the resolve to follow through on his family's needs. And all through life, our family loved each other and we loved the Lord. For this, we would be forever blessed with God's everlasting love and favors. Gary was always one step ahead of everyone. His mind was always planning and preparing to make tomorrow better than today.

Gary knew these two little girls were God's greatest gift and blessing to him. They were his considerable purpose. Gary had been given a tough but rewarding job. He had been handed the supreme highest job title given to man. The job title was "Dad." He would be successful in this never-ending job.

Gary passed away in 2019. However, he is still performing this supreme job. The girls believe their dad is still holding first place in the categorization of "Best Dad." They believe he is in heaven wearing a crown reading "Best Dad." And we can all see his proud heart and the twinkle in his beautiful kind blue eyes.

Gary's girls are surrounded by a large crowd of individuals witnessing their dad's success at his job as their dad. Gary knew he was blessed. He loved and was grateful for his family.

God was pledging to my husband he was always standing beside him, promising Gary he would never be alone, assuring Gary of his love and faithfulness.

Gary's girls are still saying to him, "Keep loving, showing, and teaching us," "We love you, honor you, and we still need you," "Dad, you have and still are giving glory to God by continuing your job as our terrific dad."

My husband left a legacy of love and kindness. Gary was the kind of man who would forgive people when others would agree forgiveness was not deserved. I sometimes would fall prey to the decision of forgiveness being unwarranted. I hate to admit on occasion I have difficulty forgiving. It is sometimes difficult because my life has presented me with always needing to protect myself from the pain of rejection and unkind words.

I never understood as a child growing up Rosiclare why some people disliked me enough to cause me so much emotional pain. Over time with the love and understanding of Gary and others, I have learned to forgive and drop my grievances toward the offender and their accomplice. I will never forget these offenders and the damage caused to my young spirit, but Jesus knew my heart. He knew I wanted to forgive them. He has given to me the peace that is received when we forgive those who have caused us pain. To those who because of their disrespect for human decency and their negative rude destructive behavior handed to us problems that would take years to control. We cannot expect God to forgive us if we cannot forgive others.

Gary was devoted to his family. He loved, protected, provided, and knew everything he did mattered to his family. As a dad, he was full of hope for his daughters. Gary loved those two little girls with all his heart and his soul. Like every good earthly father, he wanted to raise them to do great things. He knew God wanted that too. Because Gary knew God loved Stephanie and Stacy even more than he loved them, and Gary prayed for God's guidance and help with his responsibility to his girls.

Gary left a spiritual legacy to his children and grandchildren. They observed Gary's life and are influenced. He left them a legacy that can never be lost, forgotten, consumed, spent, decreased, or ignored. Gary left a legacy of knowing Jesus Christ as his savior. Leaving your family with a spiritual legacy carries the largest inheritance you will ever know to be given to anyone. Gary passed his love, his faith in God and Jesus, to his children and grandchildren. What would be learned from my husband's life is kindness and forgiveness. We sometimes forget we cannot recover our harsh words after they are spoken. And we cannot recollect the time after it is gone.

Love your family and friends. Be kind and spend as much time with them as you can. Be an example and leave a legacy they can be proud of. A legacy they will be grateful for and will honor.

Gary was my husband and he was my trusted friend. He told me to take charge of my ambitions. To give myself credit and compliment myself and my achievements big or small. He lifted my spirit with a card, a flower, or just an "I love you" or "I am proud of you." He helped me find my inner strength. He exerted much time and understanding repairing, improving, bolstering, and sustaining my confidence.

As a young girl, my heart's desire was to find my prince charming. Gary was put in my life to make my dreams come true. He was handsome, kind, and smart. I always thought of Gary as enchanting. After all, he was the man who appeared in the dreams of a little five-year-old girl, growing up in Rosiclare, shy, lonely, and abandoned. This dream was kept alive, and Gary would one day make this dream come true. Yes, my dreams of Gary—the man I would marry, my prince charming—were fanciful and imaginative. I can tell you with certainty that dreams can come true.

Gary accomplished a lot in his life. He always took the high road when circumstances in life would cause most of us to race to the bottom of the hill. Most would stay at the bottom of the hill wallowing in pity and self-destruction. Waiting for sympathy and waiting without trying to change and correct that which was brought us to this unbalanced emotional time in our life. But not my husband. He knew life brought difficulty to everyone. He knew when this happens we are the ones who have to run our way back. No one would or could do that for us. They can encourage us, provide us with advice and good counsel, and console us. But we have to do the inevitable because the conclusion to our calamity depends on us alone.

Problems in life happen to everyone. They sometimes can be avoided but problems are sure to occur. How we face life's inescapable difficulties and problems is the difference in our thriving or merely existing. No matter who you see, where you are from, who is in your life and circle of friends, no matter what you have or have not done, no matter where you live, no matter your social status or lack thereof, problems in life are popular to us all.

Gary always managed bad experiences well. He had plenty of difficult experiences in the US Navy and with his demanding career at Duke. He was always dedicated and determined to make a negative into a positive. Gary's composure was always calm, optimistic, hopeful, and in control. His confidence was filled with his unwavering, determined, decisive resoluteness. His faith led his way. Gary knew God loved him not for who he was or what he did. But God loved him for who God is. My husband never showed anger, fear, or the thought of failing. His strength was always present. A lot of his strength came from knowing he was never alone. Gary's life was so close to a mirrored image of what God does when you walk alongside Him.

My husband's bravery and faith were obvious and easily perceived by me and the girls. Even near and at the end of his life, he was showing us love and strength. He was giving us compassion when he was the one suffering.

Gary was diagnosed with dementia in late 2017. He was able to keep it from me and the girls until then. He had always been so smart, the answer to all our questions, and he was always our biggest supporter and admirer. He was where we went to find love, devotion, and compassion. He was who we went to find defense and protection from the world. And now for the first time, he was incapable of delivering on the strength we so depended on.

Before Gary passed away, the dementia had become Alzheimer's. The Alzheimer's never became really bad. He always knew me and the girls. He knew his three grandchildren but could not remember their names. Gary remained sweet and kind to the end. We believe he and Jesus were keeping close company near the end of his life. Gary did not want to cause me and the girls worry. He never wanted us to feel sad. We believe he asked God to take him before the Alzheimer's became seriously debilitating. The last month of his life, he continuously told me how much he loved me and how happy his life had been because of me. Gary told me often he loved me but never this often, repeatedly and persistently telling his two girls how much he loved them and how happy and proud they had made him. The girls and I thought it was the Alzheimer's. However, we soon learned he was telling us goodbye.

Shortly after mine and Gary's fiftieth wedding anniversary, God decided Gary had fulfilled and satisfied his plan. Gary went to be with the Lord in March 2019.

Like everything Gary did, he took good care of his health. He went for a physical every year, and the results of his physical were good. No heart problems that his doctor knew of, but Gary passed away with a massive heart attack. His passing was unexpected. Mine and the girls' hearts are broken. Our hearts will always hold the memory of a wonderful husband and father. We love him and miss him every day. Until the Alzheimer's, Gary lived a busy, active, and productive life. We know God had a strategy, a design, and a specific goal and job waiting for Gary. Gary was a doer, accomplisher, achiever, a man of action. Gary was seventy-four years of age and had so much more good to offer. When Gary passed away, we found in his shirt pocket a picture of his three grandchildren. They were all little children in the picture but at the time of his passing, they were in college and high school. He had been carrying that photo with him for many years. He had been transferring that picture of his grandchildren from one shirt pocket to another shirt and pocket. Always keeping the picture close to his heart.

We had a closed casket for Gary. However, the day before his funeral we visited for the last time on earth the husband, father, father-in-law, and granddaddy we loved, admired, respected, and would miss. Remember me telling you of Gary's beautiful blue twinkling eyes. Gary in his casket was smiling and those blue eyes were a little open and twinkling. God knew our sadness and this was his way of assuring us Gary was happy and was with him. We already knew that, but we are still very grateful to God for that sign.

Just like Pa, Gary's funeral was crowded. Our large church was full, and Gary's funeral was in the afternoon of a workday. More evidence of the love, admiration, and respect for my husband. Gary refused to allow negativity in his life. Gary responded to everyone with kindness. He never grew weary of being thoughtful and helpful.

I am thankful for the more than fifty years I shared with Gary. Gary was my champion, my shield, and my love, and he will always remain in my heart. He gave so many wonderful, happy, and unforgettable memories to my empty life. God was holding me close when he placed Gary at my side.

Gary was the most prepared person I know. Always ready and able for every challenge. Gary was prepared for eternity. My husband is now smarter, handsomer, and kinder than before. Without Gary, I feel like ninety-nine percent of me is missing. I see him every day and I talk to him every day. I love him so. Gary and I were on a journey together for over fifty years. Gary's life is about who he showed himself to be all along the way. He brought me much happiness.

He was a gift to me bestowed by God for which I am grateful. Gary would always say to me, "I will love you until the hand of time stops." Gary kept that promise. He loved me to the end. He is now in the presence of the Lord and he is still loving me.

Gary's legacy is the exemplar of human decency to all people. He showed compassion to everyone. He was genuine, and everyone saw his manners, conduct, attitude, and more distinctive qualities as his real and true character. He is my prince.

> That if thou shalt confess with thy mouth the Lord Jesus, and shalt believe in thine heart that God hath raised him from the dead, thou shalt be saved. (Romans 10:9 KJV)

Just like my favorite fairy tale, Cinderella, my fairy tale has a happy ending too! I cannot bring Gary back, but I can go to him someday. "AND THEY LIVED HAPPY EVER AFTER."

Card with red roses for my 18th birthday. Gift from my charming Gary.

Gary, my sailor. US Navy 1965

My handsome husband, Gary.

Mine and Gary's Wedding Day.

Me and Gary. Oh Happy Day.

Gary and Me.

Me and Gary.

Me and Gary at our daughter's wedding.

Me and my beloved husband, Gary.

15

God Saved My Empty Life

I would seek unto God, and unto God would I commit my cause: Which doeth great things and unsearchable; marvellous things without number. (Job 5:8, 9 KJV)

You have all read by now many times I was abandoned at six months old by both parents. God had a plan for my life. He took control of my life and kept everyone in his plan for me to walk with him. He kept them healthy in body and spirit. He kept them from falling down on the job he had given to them regarding this helpless and innocent, and abandoned baby girl. Because of God's love and the people he put in my life, I have a blessed, happy life with purpose.

Now God did not intend for me to be wealthy, have social status, be famous, or be a woman of stature having importance. But he intended to give me, if I would let him, a life and future I had been denied at birth by my offensive parents. My mother and dad's beyond-the-pale behavior toward me was outside the boundaries of acceptance. God wanted me to find love, have a family, and find, develop, and explore the God-given talent he awarded me. And I believe he wanted me to share with you this life of parental abandonment, a childhood lived alongside poor. A shy, passive life that was ignored, made to feel unimportant, and made to feel unworthy of love, kindness, and acceptance. This done by extended family, church, public school, and many acquaintances. I seemed to draw this kind of conduct and way of behaving from people. Maybe it was my life circumstances or maybe it was because I was passive and would not offer my defense. But it was apparent early in my life I would be the favorite person to ridicule and make fun of my lonely existence.

God also had something more he wanted for my life. He offered this eternal gift to me and I accepted. I accepted Jesus as my savior and what a benefit and advantage in my life it has been to know he is always with me. To know there is nothing I want to do and nothing I could do to cause him to abandon me or stop loving me. The peace of knowing Jesus and having a relationship with him is an inspiring delight. It is a divine experience, and this relationship will change how you think, act, and live. The wonders of his love and faithfulness are immeasurable.

A life to forget began with two young people, my parents. My dad was selfish, thinking only of himself in the moment. My mother was rebellious, always demanding to get her way or her wrath would express itself. They were married in July 1945. Mother was almost thirteen years old and Dad was twenty. They made their home with Mother's parents until November 1947. My grandfather, whose health was failing, worked every day supporting them while my dad remained unemployed. My dad had no intention of working, and he had no intention of taking this marriage seriously. My mother was too young, turbulent, and her behavior was always unpredictable and impossible to control.

The two years they lived with my grandparents were spent partying in the company of lively individuals. They were living a life of no responsibility. Mother and dad were escaping life through entertainment and association with people of undesirable character.

Dad was lazy. His care and concern were for nothing but partying and drinking. Mother's behavior every day was rude and abusive to everyone.

My parents caused much sadness to my grandparents the two years they lived with my Mamaw and Papaw. Mother and dad caused grandparents both mental and physical stress. My parents caused them worries and they contributed to my grandfather's decline in his health. It did not matter how good you treated mother. A person could never do enough to escape her extreme verbal abuse. She would sometimes show physical pain to my dad. Most of mother's violent temper and altercation would consist of harsh words. Almost unable to forgive was her weapon of slurs. Dad was not any better. He was irresponsible, reckless, carefree, and could not fulfill his commitments, promises, and responsibilities to this marriage. He was also abusive, but his abuse was different from mothers. Dad's abuse was neglect in every categorization of responsibility. The marriage was doomed from the beginning. I think mother married to get away from home, but that did not happen for her. It would not have mattered where my mother lived or who she lived with. Her life was always angry and confused.

I believed my dad suffered a stupid moment when he married my mother. At that time in his life and in his youth, he was immature. He was acting on impulsive behavior and dad would spend all his time escaping reality. Dad was eliminating all assignments and duty that belonged to him. His actions would prove to be incorrect, showing no obligation to anyone or anything. There was no stability, no dependability, no accountability in his inadequate functional life. Sometime later my dad's life would give a person the impression he had conformed; his life would make you think he had become an acceptable husband and father to his second family. This lifestyle never would happen for my mother.

In November 1947, mother and dad moved to Waukegan, Illinois. They took me with them. Three months later, in February

1948, they separated. Mother, with me, returned to Rosiclare to live with my Mamaw and Papaw. But Mother did not stay in Rosiclare. She moved to Griffin, Indiana, and dad stayed in Waukegan. When they took me to Waukegan at three months old, Mamaw had been taking care of me. I was a healthy baby. Mother and Dad had me for three months of my life. When mother brought me back to Rosiclare at six months, I had to seek a doctor. I had lost a lot of weight, had a cold, fever, and was dehydrated. Mamaw nursed me back to good health. My poor health was a direct result of the neglect of my parents.

When mother left for Griffin, Indiana, she did not ask grand-parents if she could leave me. It did not matter to her because her personality would allow her to always think only of herself. Mother left, giving my grandparents the responsibility of laboring what to do with this baby girl. Dad was nowhere to be found. He was missing. All my life dad remained missing and never made himself available to me. Never giving or offering help or concern.

Still a baby, the idea of adoption gave hope to my mother of being rid of me forever. My dad had already made the decision to eliminate me from all emotion, attachment, and all other aspects of his life. My dad had made the decision to discard me and dismiss me as of no value and no existence. But, as already discussed, because of the crying and begging of Mamaw and Uncle Ben, mother at the last minute decided against my adoption. Mother took off to Griffin, Indiana, again to work and live. I was left at my grandparents' house by mother. I do not remember my grandfather because he passed away when I was twenty-one months old. I only know of his good-ness and the honorable man he was, as shared with me by Mamaw and others.

When my grandfather passed away, Mamaw took me and we went to live with her widowed father and old maid sister. These two precious souls were my great-grandfather, Pa, and my great-aunt

Lottie. Pa and Aunt Lottie were happy we would be living with them. They welcomed us with much love and much warm acceptance.

Life would offer to me what I needed. I did not have a lot of the extras other children had, but I always had the necessities. I never wanted much or asked for much. Therefore, all my life it never occurred to me we were living a life of modest means. A life of less monetary and no financial comfort unlike all other Rosiclare. The only other home I had been in growing up Rosiclare was my friend, Carole. Her house was beautifully furnished, but I gave it no thought. Pa's house, now my house, had plastic curtains, linoleum floor covering, and all furniture was bought at the secondhand furniture store. All sofas and chairs were covered with a sheet to hide the tears in the fabric. The tears were there when we bought the furniture. Because my Mamaw washed and ironed for people to support me, clothes were hung to dry in the living room all winter. We had a big, ugly potbelly coal stove that only kept the living room warm. We had no vehicle and we walked everywhere we went. We walked to church, the grocery store, and downtown.

There was so much love in my home with Mamaw, Pa, and Aunt Lottie. They loved me very much. I believe their purpose for living was to make sure I had a fair chance in life. Because of them, I did have a chance of a good happy life and I did not disappoint them. The words *mother* and *dad* were never spoken in my house. I was in first grade at school before I gave attention to and noticed my life was drastically different from other children. All my time growing up I never asked questions. There was never a discussion regarding why I was being raised by these three old people. As I became older, I would hear Uncle Ben talking to my grandmother about me and my parents. And of course, on my mother's visits, she would always bring up every small detail of her life. She always blamed everyone for the troubled life she was living. This is how I learned much of my abandonment. Mother seemed to have no regret and never gave me attention or even talked to me on her visits to Rosiclare. She was almost as absent as my dad. As I grew older, I was often the conversation when Ben and Mother came to Rosiclare for a visit. This conversation was never started by my Mamaw. It was always a conversation she never wanted to take part in. And of course, Uncle Ben and mother's conversation regarding me was always negative. They never gave my Mamaw one red penny to help her support me. I do not know why they felt obligated to cause me emotional stress. Ben was bitter because Mamaw was having to raise me. Mother was always condescending, arrogant, and always treated Mamaw with irreverence. Some of Ben's visits and most all mother's visits left my grandmother hurt and burdened. Their visits contributed to my already broken spirit and low self-esteem.

I will talk often of my classmates. However, I want to make myself clear, and I want all to know only a very few classmates were mean to me. Only a very few classmates bullied me with words and emotional intimidation. Still, throughout all public school, I was seen yet unseen. My days at school were lonely. The first time I realized my life was different from other children was first grade. My first-grade class gave a program. Mothers were invited. All the children's mothers attended, as did my Mamaw. After the program, Miss J asked the children to introduce their mother to the class. As a six-year-old that day, I noticed everyone's mother was young, beautiful, and picture-perfect groomed. These mothers could have been described as wearing pretty, young, and fashionable attire. That day, my Mamaw was dressed in old-fashioned, matronly appearing garments. The person in attendance representing me was my grandmother, and she was old.

That was the day I knew my life was different. My young classmates must have noticed and questioned too. I went all through the Rosiclare Public School, kindergarten through grade 12, being ignored and forgotten. Throughout my youth, I was always quiet, shy, and passive. I was too little then to understand, even in first grade, why I was treated differently by my classmates. They would never involve me enough for me to make a friend. Later, I would realize I was mistreated because they knew my cultural background was different from theirs.

At six years old, these young children already knew my life situation was not acceptable in Rosiclare society. The way they would handle this problem with my cultural identity would be isolation. I was identified as being different. I did not have a proper family. I did not have a mother and dad who loved, protected, and made a home for me. I did not understand their reasoning for this treatment at six years old. I had a home and three people who loved me. I was learning my life was not like theirs. My life was not the standard, but that was no reason to make me invisible. Mother and dad were words unknown to me. I had no acquaintance, no experience, and no familiarity with the words *mother* and *dad*. Those words did not exist in my little life and my little world.

In school, I was always made to feel I was guilty of something. Made to feel I was not worthy of their acceptance. I remember being on the playground, standing alone, and watching the others have fun. They were not going to welcome me to play with them. I was different to them. They thought of me as not being their equal. Early in life, I would have to accept this kind of treatment and feelings directed to me by students of Rosiclare schools. The situation would never improve and only worsen as the students became older, more brazen, and undaunted. I would soon learn their entertainment was keeping me isolated and in solitude. I never discussed this with my grandmother or anyone. I kept everything inside until long into my adult years. Maybe if I had stood up for myself and showed courage and confidence, I could have put a stop to their insensitive behavior. Maybe if I had HELD MY HEAD HIGH! But I did not. The longer always being left alone continued, the more insecure, helpless, and emotionally scarred I became. My years spent in Rosiclare schools proved to be sad and lonely. I began to believe this was how I was supposed to be treated. I began to believe I was not their equal and not worthy of their friendship. Children can be deliberately unkind, indifferent, and unconcerned with the child known to be deprived of the family, advantages, and resources they considered necessary for acceptance. They can be deliberately spiteful and callous.

This treatment of me by some of my classmates through all the grades in school stayed with me my entire life. It still causes me hurt and anxiety today. They made me feel I was not good enough; they picked on me, preyed on me, and brought attention to what they considered my undesirable and unnatural family. All this added to my insecurities and lack of confidence. Their actions destroyed my ability to function, making me emotionally and mentally weak. My young passive, subdued personality made it impossible for me to adapt, accept, or change them and their contempt for me. Therefore, my entire time in school was spent allowing them to damage my usefulness and faith in myself. In those days I gave no response, no argument, and no resistance. I have come a long way. I would never tolerate their bad and inhumane behavior today.

My time at school was sad, and I disliked school very much. I never told my grandmother or anyone I disliked school or why. I never complained or whined in all those years. Over the years, I learned to stay out of everyone's way.

All my classmates knew I was being raised by a grandmother. In their minds, they may have thought if my parents did not like me, why should they like me. Rosiclare in the 1950s and 1960s had almost no broken families. Mothers and dads did not give away their baby. Classmates had total disregard for me. They passed over me for all activities, shrugged me off, snubbed, shunned, and excluded me always. Even though I had the love and affection of my Mamaw, Pa, and Aunt Lottie. I had my best friend Carole and her parents. My life was still painful, experiencing sorrow, rejection, and isolation by many individuals. Some in my extended family. All this was out of the control of the people who loved me. All they could do to aid me was love me more. They each assisted greatly in this type of help. They were unable to fix my problems, but because of their never growing tired of me, I went from a nobody and became a somebody. THEY NEVER QUIT—THEY NEVER GAVE UP.

I lived behind the grade school. The playground was in front of my house. Classmates would see my grandmother hanging clothes on the clothesline. They would see my elderly great-grandfather working in the yard and the garden. They would see Great-Aunt Lottie sweeping off the front porch. They knew this was my home and my family. They recognized my family had no similarities to their family and the family of their friends. It was determined I was their outcast. They made me into a child who belonged nowhere. These classmates all through my public school attendance would thrust me out of their society, refused to accept me, and refused to even give me a chance. I was disliked, rejected, and degraded for nothing I had done. I was alienated by everyone. I was avoided, made fun of, and made to feel like a stranger to kids I would know all my youth in Rosiclare.

All this rejection and ridicule would be a major contributor to my feeling of worthlessness and the destruction of my emotions. I was treated by these kids as always being absent and missing. Again I was made to know I had been abandoned, deserted and had no existence. This caused me to become more withdrawn. I was afraid for many years to communicate with anyone for fear of rejection and hurt. I remained very quiet, detached, introverted, and shy until many, many years later. However, when I did finally come out of my so-called happy place of an empty shell, I came blazing. I had at last become the woman and made the life for myself that my Mamaw had sacrificed so much to give. The life she prayed for and through her faith knew would be achieved. She knew the fulfillment she visualized of my good life would one day come to fruition.

I was in second grade. Uncle Ben had given to me a white rabbit named Snowball. Remember the grade school playground was directly in front of my house. With the permission of my teacher and my grandmother, I invited my second-grade classmates to my house. I wanted to introduce them to my beautiful white rabbit. Pa had made Snowball a cage. He had lots of rabbit food waiting for the children to feed this little creature. That day Mamaw had clothesline strung up all over our living room. She had clothes hanging up to dry. And then there was that ugly cast iron potbelly coal stove. My classmates saw this and their young impressionable and easily persuaded minds went into operation. Their so-called switch had been turned on. The classmates' memory of their visit to my house had been ignited never to burn itself out. They noticed my family, my home, and its furnishings were much different from theirs. I knew no different. I was a little girl and I was proud of my family and my home. I never again invited any school children to my house.

I always had everything I needed. And I had dolls, a bicycle, a rabbit, and my dog, Dover. Mamaw, Pa, and Aunt Lottie never made me feel we were poor. They never indicated we were living a meager life, limited and lacking in the amount of quantity to all other Rosiclare families. Even though my self-esteem was damaged at school, my family made me feel loved, wanted, and accepted at home. Mamaw, Pa, and Aunt Lottie raised me to believe I was everyone's equal. They told me I could do and be all my heart desired. I learned much later as an adult, this encouragement, foresight, and truth had resonated. I was a young child, but I was listening. When I finished school and got away from the negativities of being Rosiclare, I was reminded often of their teaching.

Their voices of wisdom still echo in my mind. My life has been aligned with theirs. I share their feelings of all things significant. I will learn in my adult years Mamaw, Pa, and Aunt Lottie's treatment of me will have a lasting promising emotional effect on me. It will be stronger, outlive the disturbing treatment, and emotional suffering directed to me all through my school years. Mamaw, Pa, and Aunt Lottie made a firm commitment to God regarding my upbringing. They all were determined to not let anyone or anything stop them from honoring God with the difficult task he had blessed their lives in giving them me to raise. They taught me all through my young life while in their care the same lesson. They would instruct to have integrity, go to school, work hard, save your money. Play by the rules, be kind, have courage, and always make Jesus the biggest part of my life. They were most definitely three wise individuals. They never altered or gave up on that lesson. They believed it. It is a lesson for all to follow and share.

I ask God often why he favored me so much. Why he loved and protected me. Allowed me to be able to share with you the good people in my life. I don't deserve even one of his many blessings. I have done nothing to earn his love. I have at times toppled and stumbled, but he was always there to catch me. I am not worthy of and not entitled to, but God would NEVER QUIT—NEVER GAVE UP on me and his plan for me.

Mother had two more children. Her second husband was twenty-one years her senior. Together they had a girl and a boy. They divorced when the girl was fourteen and the boy was eleven years old. The children chose to live with their dad, and they would have nothing to do with their mother, my mother. They were both estranged from her the remainder of their life. The daughter passed away at the age of thirty-five from diabetes. Mother's son passed away at the age of forty-nine from a brain aneurysm. They had no children. My two daughters are my mother's only grandchildren. Of my mother's three children, I was the only one given a chance. Mother's other two children's lives were sad and bitter, same as her life.

One Halloween in the seventh grade, all classmates came to school wearing costumes. Every student but me had been recognized and had removed their mask. I was the only classmate left standing. The teacher asked the students to guess the lone classmate still in costume and mask. No one was able to say it was me. That was always my life at school. Always forgotten, always overlooked. Always seen but never seen.

I am still in Rosiclare grade school. The grade school was kindergarten through eighth grade. I was not only treated with hostility and emotions of offensive hateful behavior from classmates but received this treatment from a few teachers too. During the '50s and '60s, Rosiclare schools and one teacher too and classmates put individuals in categories. If a person was decided to the wrong category, they were treated with unfriendliness, disapproval, disgust, annoyance, and other like unacceptable conduct. I had a teacher while still in grade school who treated me poorly. The teacher had placed me in an unacceptable category all by myself. On one memorable occasion the teacher showed classmates their purposeful intent to disrespect me and my family. Anyone and especially a schoolteacher who did what this teacher did to promote the already disfavor and dislike of classmates directed toward me is a show of their character. A show of the real person they choose to be. The teacher was shameless in their cruel behavior that day. The teacher received loud laughter and approval from students. My classmates undoubtedly agreed with our deplorable teacher.

The back wall of my classroom was all windows. One day my great-grandfather Uncle John was seen walking to town. Uncle John, my Pa, was in his late eighties in age. He was bent forward somewhat at the shoulders. Pa's posture was slumped some because of hard work and age. The teacher knew Uncle John was my great-grandfather and was helping to raise me. The teacher had been to my house because Mamaw babysat for their small child. The teacher walked around the classroom that day mocking, laughing, and imitating my Pa's slumped shoulders and walk. Of course, the classmates roared with laughter for they were being entertained at my expense. I remember putting my head down, being sad, embarrassed, and wiping away my tears. The truth be known, my teacher had much respect for Uncle John as all residents of Rosiclare. However, for some reason, teacher felt necessary to mock my great-grandfather.

My great-grandfather never mocked, never made fun of, or was never hurtful to anyone. Uncle John's greatest sin that day was being my Pa. I never told anyone about the hurtful incident and show of superiority regarding me and Pa. However, when my teacher would

162

come to my house to get Mamaw to babysit, I always made sure not to be seen. For a very long time I recognized and remembered this teacher as being a puffed-up, sanctimonious, and insincere individual. Because you understand, my teacher had deliberately, consciously, and intentionally made fun of and mocked someone I loved very much. An old man who was kind and good to everyone. This was someone who loved me with all his heart.

I imagine my teacher and Miss X, you will learn of her next, had some emotional issues with their own inferiority. These types of people always find it necessary to ridicule and humiliate others. It gives them a feeling of importance and a feeling of being better than the person they are causing hurt. We should feel pity for these people. The hurt they are suffering because of who they chose to be is greater than the hurt they caused me or you. The action my teacher took that day fueled my classmates. In the '50s and '60s, unlike today, people kept things to themselves. They did not share personal hurt like people do today. I never confided this to anyone.

The actions of my teacher that day were emotional abuse and bullying directed toward me. The teacher humiliated and insulted me. The teacher disrespected an old man only because they could. There would be no one to hold the teacher accountable for the mockery and disdain of an old man. There would be no one to defend my great-grandfather. This added to my already loneliness, anxiety, and social unacceptance by my classmates. Maybe the teacher showed disrespect to Pa because of envy and jealousy. Uncle John had the respect of all Rosiclare. One of the many reasons Uncle John was respected and admired by all: Uncle John would never subject anyone to the dishonor, arrogant, humiliating conduct awarded him that day. My teacher gave no appearance of being ashamed for their actions. As for me, my teacher severely injured their dignity that day. I would no longer respect or like this teacher and I was glad when the school year ended. This was the constant kind of belittling I was forced to endure all through public school. All because my home and

163

family were not like theirs. I was decided to be not that fortunate; my designated category was different from theirs.

There was a hurtful and mean girl in my class. She would remain in my classes all through school. In the presence of other classmates and children, she would say unkind things to me. She would bully me and make fun of me. I was so passive and would offer no defense. This lack of action from me empowered her and kept her mistreatment of me alive. The other classmates always stood in amusement. They did not hassle me; however, they offered me no help. They never once came to my rescue.

This girl, we will call her Miss X, made sure I was the last one picked to be on a sports team in PE class. She made sure I was excluded from every activity. Miss X wanted more than anything to be popular. I suppose belittling me made her feel superior and a favorite with her classmates. They were not mean to me the way Miss X was; however, they all would appear influenced, inspired, and entertained by her almost intolerable behavior directed at me. The classmates' total indifference for me was apparent and easily recognized. Miss X would be the winner. All through school, she would be popular. All through school, I would be the outcast.

Miss X every day showed contempt for me. She bullied me, expressed deep dislike and disapproval of me for no reason other than this was her character. She also behaved this way because my home life was different from the others. I had no mother or dad and was being raised by a poor grandmother. The refusal of classmates to associate with me, to be supportive of me in shaming Miss X to stop harassing me destroyed my self-esteem. These youths made me feel that my entire time in the public schools of Rosiclare, I was too different from them to be noticed. These classmates could be called followers. Because their failure in stopping Miss X delighted in helping her make me feel disgusting, detested, and despised. Classmates' no action in defending me against Miss X helped grow my strong feeling of my value and self-worth to be less than zero.

I took Miss X's mistreatment and abuse and told no one and complained to no one. My life at school and the isolation I experienced was almost unbearable. Because of Miss X., I always had a strong dislike for school. This cruel and aloneness I was made to endure at school contributed greatly, even today, to my inability to make friends. It added to my feelings of being unworthy. It most likely contributed to my being only an average student in school. It caused me emotional sadness, self-criticism, and fear of rejection. It caused me social trauma with respect to fear of being negatively judged and disliked. I am still afraid to open up and socialize with others for fear of disapproval. Those years in school caused deep-rooted feelings of self-doubt. I always feel the need to take the blame for everything. My self-esteem was destroyed. I placed no value on my life. That is why today I try so hard at everything. I must prove my worth and capabilities. I have to prove my classmates were wrong. Everyone is different. My personality was perfect for Miss X to control and destroy much of my youth. I was timid and weak. If I had been a loud, boisterous, rowdy, high-spirited, or animated child, the mistreatment might never have occurred. I was an easy target. A child already wounded by my parents. I made school fun and rewarding for Miss X. I made Miss X's job of managing me easy. If I had stayed in Rosiclare after graduation, I would have gone nowhere in my life. Always believing I was a nobody. It is difficult to outperform the perception a person has of themselves. But I did! Later in life, I would show strength, great energy, and enthusiasm and would come out like a real trooper. It took a long time, but God and the people in my life would at last reach their goal for me.

I would tell myself if I ever saw Miss X after graduation, I would inflict on her some of the punishment she had given me year after year. I did see her several times on my visits to Rosiclare. However, I could never bring myself to act hurtful toward her. I did what I always did regarding Miss X. I stayed out of her way. When people act like Miss X, they have their own insecurities. Acting the way they do gets all attention off their fears. Miss X was afraid of being exposed for her weakness. Her panic feelings of wanting to be liked and her anxiety about having to be popular. Miss X knew she was wearing a mask. She knew she was portraying herself to be tough and strong. But in all certainty she knew herself to be an always frightened person, easily injured, and always tormented about social acceptance. By disparaging me, she kept her true identity from her classmates never to be exposed for her helpless and needy character. She kept her alarm from sounding, deceiving herself and others. I did not realize at the time, but Miss X was probably as sad and unhappy as she made me.

To my knowledge, I was the only child in Rosiclare schools in the 1950s and 1960s, and until I graduated, that was raised by a grandmother. I never dated in high school. I had no girlfriends in school; therefore, I would surely have no boyfriends. I started babysitting at thirteen years old. I babysat every Friday and Saturday night until I left Rosiclare. Most of my customers were my teachers or Alcoa Executive employees. I made 50¢ an hour, and my fee changed to 60¢ an hour after midnight. This was from 1960 through May 1965. I always saved my babysitting money. I always managed to have enough to buy new school clothes at the beginning of the new school year. I would only spend my earned money taking Uncle Ben's little boys to the movie theater every Sunday they visited. On Sunday mornings, I would give God his rightful share of my weekend babysitting remuneration.

Regrettably, I remember trying to make change in the offering plate one Sunday morning; I was wanting to take from the offering plate the difference in God's 10 percent and the change I had on my person. Very unfortunate for me, Mamaw witnessed me making change. She did not approve of my hand being in the offering plate taking money. She let it be known I would never try that maneuvering scheme again. I felt so embarrassed and ashamed of my selfish insulting actions that day to God who had given to me so much. To this day, my hand is in the offering plate to give never to take. This was back in the day when people dropped coins and dollar bills in the church offering.

Uncle Ben, Aunt Joan, and their two little boys were at our house every other Sunday for the noon meal. Rosiclare had a movie theater. Carole and I went every Sunday afternoon. Tickets were 25¢, and a Coke and bag of popcorn were 5¢ each. We always took my two little cousins to the movies. I had to use my babysitting money to buy their movie ticket and their refreshments. Ben and Joan loved money so much they would not pay for their little boys' trip to the movies. Instead, they watched me spend my earned babysitting money. I never thought anything about Ben and Joan's greed and insensitivity. I do not know why. I loved my little cousins. I may have been too naive to grasp what was taking place. Maybe God took from me the ability and the desire to notice Uncle Ben and Aunt Joan's unfair and selfish love of money. It took me years to notice this. God protected me from recognizing this uncaring, hard-hearted nature of Uncle Ben. A man I still loved and remembered the time gone when his heart showed goodness and benevolence. I loved my extended family regardless of how they treated me.

As I grew older, I came to know and understand the circumstances of my existence. Unfortunately, I did become hard and critical of my extended family. They all treated me as a mistake. They all thought of me and treated me as an unwelcome, uninvited, nauseating leech and moocher. I was never a burden to any of my extended family except the three old people who raised me. All other extended family never gave me anything and would not acknowledge me as family. They disliked my parents and regrettably they had good reason. They were angered and jealous that Mamaw was supporting me. I wonder how much of her $20 a week they thought they would receive if she did not need to spend it on me. Without those three elderly people who raised me, my life would have been in ruin, collapse, and total shatter. As I grew older and accepted Jesus Christ as my savior, I had to ask for help in forgiving some family and others. I was much stubborn with giving my forgiveness. My heart had been severely torn and it took me a long time to forgive. I am not proud of that truth. Thankfully, I have forgiven them. I will never forget but I have forgiven. Remember too, the Bible says we will not be forgiven of our sins if we cannot forgive those who have sinned against us. I do believe remembering helps keep us strong and determined.

One of my babysitting customers was a teacher's family. They were Friday night regulars for three or four years. Mr. and Mrs. B belonged to a square dance club. The dance club met every Friday night. They had four young children. One summer they made plans to go to the Big Du Quoin fair in Du Quoin, Illinois. They asked Mamaw if I could go with them. She said I could. I remember being so excited. I had never been anywhere. I just knew this trip to the big fair would be exciting and fun. The trip to the fair turned out to be a babysitting job. I was asked to go because they needed me to watch and care for their one-year-old while everyone else enjoyed the fair. I carried a one-year-old baby girl around while they all rode the rides, were made happy, and were entertained. I did not have the opportunity to play a game or enjoy any of the amusement rides. Again God had complete control, for I never gave much thought to this particular situation and what it had been about until much later in my life. I just accepted not belonging and always being treated like a second-class person. This was God protecting me. This was part of his plan for me. He was making me strong. Mr. and Mrs. B meant no harm. They were just like most everyone else. I did not need to have fun. I was just a poor abandoned child who needed their babysitting job to survive. My high school years were spent in class and going to some of the home basketball games. And of course, my high school years suffered the torment and anguish delivered to me daily by Miss X.

I graduated high school in June 1965. The next day, an extended family member, my mother's cousin, had been visiting his family in Rosiclare. On his way home to Kenosha, Wisconsin, he agreed to take me to Jacksonville, Illinois. He took me to the home of a second cousin I had met only once. I needed to leave Rosiclare to have any kind of a life and future. There were no job opportunities in Rosiclare. Both my mother and Uncle Ben lived thirty miles from the big city of Evansville, Indiana. There would have been opportunities for me in Evansville; however, neither one of them offered to help me. Mamaw gave me $50 to take to Jacksonville. My second cousin let me live with her and her family for seven weeks. I paid them $10 a week, but they wanted me to find a new place to live. My second cousin and her family were very good to me. I am grateful to them for their help. I moved into one room at the Castle. Found a secretarial job quickly. It was a one-girl office which I enjoyed. I had two men bosses and enjoyed working for both of them. One of them in particular was so funny and kept me laughing. I babysat for the other boss. He had two little boys and he and his wife were great people. They always told me if they ever had a little girl, they would want her to be like me. That pleased me and made me proud. I walked 14 blocks to work every morning and 14 blocks to the Castle in the evening. I did this from July 1965 to March 1966. I did not mind the walk. In March 1966, I bought a new 1966 red Volkswagen Beetle. It cost $1,350 back then, and my car payment was $45 a month. I was eighteen years old, and the car dealership told me because of my age, I needed a cosignatory. I shared with them I did not have anyone who could cosign for me. They sold me the car anyway. That first weekend I went to Rosiclare. I had not seen Mamaw, Pa, and Aunt Lottie since I left after graduation. It had been nine months. I was so happy to see them and they were happy to see me. Rosiclare was a three-and-a-half-hour drive, and gas was 33¢ per gallon. I stayed at the same job until I married.

My life was about to experience a big change. A good change would be happening. I was going to fall in love with the boy I would marry. His name would be Gary. You could say I was going to hit the jackpot. My jackpot would not hold gold. Instead, it would be filled with love. God's plan for my life was about to take a new and different direction. My Mamaw was right, dreams can come true. I had dreamed of a prince charming since I was five years old. God had found him for me. I loved this young man with all my heart, and we shared more than fifty years together.

I met Gary in August 1965. I was eating lunch with Karen. She was renting a room at the Castle too. We were enjoying burgers at

Top's Big Boy. Karen was meeting her boyfriend. When he arrived, he brought with him a friend. His friend was Gary. Gary asked me for a date. Our first date was August 10, 1965.

We discussed getting married. I continued working and saving my money. I wanted a church wedding. My wedding was small and modest but it was again what I had wished and dreamed. We waited until after Gary's first patrol at sea before getting married. The US Navy did not pay much; however, his income did increase after his first patrol at sea. Again, his wise and cautious mind was at work. He said he wanted to be sure he could afford financially to be married.

We were married on January 26, 1969, in Jacksonville. It was a Sunday because I had asked Uncle Ben to give me away. He agreed but told me the wedding would need to take place on Sunday. The reason being, he did not want to take Friday off from work for the rehearsal. Jacksonville was a three-hour drive for him. My wedding cost less than $1,000. I paid for all of my wedding on my own. I even paid for Ben and Joan's hotel room following the rehearsal. Uncle Ben brought Mamaw but Aunt Lottie became ill and was not able to attend. Pa had passed away two weeks prior to my wedding. Mother and her third husband attended. She was estranged from her other two children; therefore, they did not attend. Gary and I were married in the church where we both were members. It was also his family's church.

I had my prince. I had my church wedding and I was very happy. We would soon be on our way to beautiful historical Charleston, South Carolina. At that time Charleston was home to a large naval base and shipyard. The nuclear submarine Gary was assigned was stationed in Charleston.

Gary was saved and accepted Jesus Christ as his savior on June 16, 1956, while attending Vacation Bible School. When Gary passed away, my son-in-law cleaned out Gary's garage. He found a small suitcase stuffed with all the letters I wrote Gary when he was in the Navy. He had kept them all.

Even though I was raised in church and always attended regularly, I did not become a Christian until I was twenty-one years old. I remember being saved like it happened only yesterday. Gary was in Charleston preparing for his first patrol at sea. I went to church every Sunday. About a month before I was saved, I would leave the church service before it was over. I would leave crying and under conviction. The Holy Spirit was present and had hold of me. However, I was too stubborn to walk down the aisle and surrender my life to Jesus. I had told my daughters I was saved around the end of September 1968. I could not remember the exact date. The morning I was saved, the Holy Spirit pushed me out of the pew and down the aisle. I was trying God's patience, and he was growing tired. God is patient and gracious to us, wanting everyone to repent.

My son-in-law brought the suitcase of letters I had written to Gary into the house. Gary had saved them each and every one. I placed the suitcase of letters in the closet. I told myself that when my grieving for the loss of Gary had lessened, I would read some of them. God's timing is so perfect. About a year ago I was feeling sad and alone missing Gary. I thought I would read a few of my old love letters I had written Gary more than fifty-five years ago. I opened the suitcase and grabbed seven letters off the top at random. I gave no conscious method or prearranged order of quickly taking hold of the seven letters from the old suitcase. I put a rubber band around them and placed them in my desk drawer. A couple of weeks later, I took the letter off the top and read it. That was the letter I had written Gary on Sunday afternoon, October 6, 1968, advising him I was saved that morning in church.

I still have not read any of the remaining letters I grabbed that day. It would be too painful for me to read. But God allowed me to read the most important letter. The small suitcase is stuffed with my letters and God controlled the one he wanted me to read. God is sovereign, and he gave his grace to me that Sunday morning. With his grace, I was saved. I needed to read that letter I wrote Gary so many years earlier. We can trust God's timing to be never early and never late, but to reinforce his plan for our life. I tried to ignore God that Sunday morning. I tried my best to shut him out. I had always been good at ignoring and had lots of experience of pushing away feelings. I was experiencing hard to control emotions those Sunday mornings. I was under conviction; however, I was going to manage this situation like I did all other awkward and stressful happenings in my life. I walked out of church many Sunday mornings and told no one. But God was having no part of my obstinate and unyielding attitude and behavior directed toward him. God pushed me down the church aisle that October morning, and I accepted Jesus as my savior. I was baptized a couple of weeks later. Now I could tell my daughters the exact day of my salvation.

You are probably wondering how a second cousin I hardly knew let me come stay with her family in Jacksonville. Again, God in charge. I knew I had to leave Rosiclare to have a life. I was so shy. I don't know how I had the nerve to ask for her help. I am glad I did because she said yes. Her mother, deceased, was Mamaw's sister, and they were very close. Maybe that is why she agreed to help me. I had spunk and a willpower I had not yet discovered. It is ironic, is it not, what you would expect that I would go to someone I did not know and ask for help. It would seem logical and within reason I would ask mother or Uncle Ben for help. I knew them. They had been part of my extended family and they both visited my home in Rosiclare all through my youth. I did not ask for their help because I knew they did not want to help me. They knew I needed them, and they offered me no support or assistance. I did not realize God was planning, guiding my life. He would let me achieve my dreams and let me achieve goals I did not yet know. God would be taking me from a life of nonexistent to a life of belonging. God had Gary waiting for me.

Gary bought me my first steak. Growing up, Rosiclare beefsteak was not in our $20-a-week food budget. I ate good as a child. Lots of beans and garden vegetables. Gary took me to a steak house restaurant when we were dating. We doubled with Gary's brother and his date. The waitress asked everyone for their order. I was glad she asked for my order last. I had never been to a nice restaurant. I was not familiar with the steak choices that were available. Everyone ordered filet mignon. When the waitress asked me for my decision, I told her I would have what they ordered. I had not heard of filet mignon. I could not pronounce it either.

Aunt Joan's mother and dad had several farms they rented to others. They were paid rent. They would receive as part payment for renting their land grown vegetables from their tenant's farm. Joan's parents owned Angus cattle they butchered and sold. This was a profitable business for Joan's dad. They also had pigs and chicken. A couple of times a year, Aunt Joan's parents would butcher an Angus cow and give it to Ben and Joan. They would also give Ben a pig and chickens. Uncle Ben would visit our house, and the trunk of his car would be full of meat. He would have steak, beef and pork roast, ribs, ground beef, ham, bacon, pork chops, and chicken. All this meat was a gift from Joan's parents. They also processed the meat for her. The meat in the trunk of her car was ready to cook. Ben would always insist that my Mamaw, his mother, would see what all they had been given. I would go to the car also to have a look. Not one time did he ever give his mother anything for all those Sunday fried chicken dinners he and his family enjoyed at my house. Ben's selfish greed was unconscionable. His lack of human decency, the absence of doing what is right, the show of pride, and his boasting of all he had been given was a show of no respect to his mother. Uncle Ben's good conscience was dead. He could feel no guilt and no regret for his indifference.

Ben was so blinded with greed he was unaware his mother's heart was aching with sadness and pity for her son. You understand Uncle Ben did not have Jesus. Ben was always hostile and belligerent when discussing Jesus. As I told you, that did not serve him well the last couple years of his life. Ben lived all his life unwisely and foolishly, denying Jesus as his savior. He denied God to the end. Do not misunderstand, for I do not think Uncle Ben should have given away much of his family's meat, all things considered, a little something once in a while for dinner would have been a show of compassion and love. My memory of Ben and Joan is their selfish desire for more money. Their insatiable greed.

I had planned to let my ninety-six-year-old great-grandfather, Pa, who helped raise me, walk me down the aisle. Pa's health appeared good, and his mind was satisfactory. However, Pa passed away three weeks before Gary and I were married. I was so proud of that old man. The only thing he accomplished was raising his big family. Mamaw was a product of his raising. He showed them how to live an honorable life. He gave his love with self-dedication to each of them. He never showed anger. Pa and Gary did not let life circumstances upset them. You cannot say that about many people. You cannot say that about me.

Mine and Gary's first child, daughter Stephanie, was born in Charleston. I went to work almost as soon as we arrived in Charleston. We could use the extra money. Navy pay was not much, but we always managed. I worked until Stephanie was ready to make herself known to me and Gary. A beautiful little girl who would grow up exhibiting much of Gary's personality and his distinctive character. To our delight and surprise, another beautiful little girl, Stacy, made her introduction to us thirteen months later. This little girl, Stacy, would also make evident she had been also blessed with a lot of Gary's inherent good qualities and his strong constitution. We felt so blessed with our family. I was not a perfect mother, none of us are; however, I always knew I was a good mother. Mamaw showed me and taught me how I was to walk these new untraveled unfamiliar miles God had granted me.

It was October 1972. Gary's seven-year tour with the Nuclear Navy was finished. We were on our way back to beautiful South Carolina. He had accepted a position at Duke Energy's big nuclear power plant. We bought our first small home. We settled into what would be over forty-four years with Duke Energy living in South Carolina.

Our two daughters would graduate college, marry local boys, and we would be also blessed with three grandchildren. Our family has always been close and connected. We are all blessed to live in the same town and see each other often. Gary and I approve and are proud of our daughters' Godly husbands. My life is evidence. God's love never fails and never abandons. The day my Mamaw's arms reached out for me was the day my little life was no longer empty. I would hold the love of my grandmother all my life. Always remembering and never forgetting her devotion, love, and sacrifice. Always giving thanks to Jesus for his love and protection. Always keeping his hand in mine so I would follow through with his plan. I tried to injure his plan a few times. But God loved me enough to always hold me close and keep me filled with energy, hope, and conviction. I did not achieve this good life. It is a gift from God. He wants a good life for you too.

I worked in an office most of our married life. Never making much money. However, in 1978 I went to work for an independent insurance agency. I had come a long way with my personality. I was beginning to experience some confidence. I was now more competitive than previously, growing up in Rosiclare. I always had to prove myself worthy and equal to everyone. I tried being competitive in school when classmates rarely involved me, but my efforts always failed. I had the security of Gary's love, and my nature, disposition, and individuality were changing. I was no longer quiet, shy, and passive. I guess you could say I evolved gradually into another individual. I could recognize this drastic change in me, and so could Gary. We both agreed this change was better.

Little by little, I was gaining faith in my abilities. I was seeing a glimpse of optimism. Surviving growing up in Rosiclare proved my courage. I was relentless, remaining dedicated and determined to achieve. Before, I had always lived my life in fear and doubt, always believing I could never measure up to anyone. But now, all my Mamaw taught me, her guidance and instruction, were about to be put to use. She had taught me how to have an opinion, how to make a decision, and how to end my conclusion. Mamaw showered me with her collection of life's standards—standards that would prove to lead me to the good life. Mamaw's goal for me would be a success. It would take years to be realized and accomplished. She would see in my life the progress and the results of all her wisdom, energy, and attention given to the granddaughter she loved so dearly.

Mamaw suffered many personal struggles caused by raising me. I witnessed many times when everything in her life was working against her. Everyone contributed negative thoughts and actions they believed would result in her failing. I watched and heard my mother many times show terrible anger, speak verbal abuse, and sound off with condescending remarks. I observed Uncle Ben's pride, greed, idolatry to be the source of his lost soul causing my grandmother deep emotional grief. Her two children she loved had disheartened her. The daughter was extremely defiant and unmanageable. The son, in love with money, resisted to acknowledge Jesus Christ. She had been a good mother, but her children now owned the proficiency of self-destruction. But my grandmother kept her faith. She never quit, never resigned, and never lost hope. I observed her strength daily. She would be the starting point of my inner strength as I became older and was on my own.

I was changing, but it would not happen overnight. I still had feelings of not belonging, of being inferior, and being of no importance. But with Gary's love and support, I was able to keep a lot of these insecurities from being noticed. I became good at my cover-up. Gradually and inch by inch, I would be surprised and stunned at the change in my disposition. I would recognize this new disposition was inborn but would take years to cultivate.

But even so, I would always have issues from being abandoned as an infant. I would forgive, but it is not necessary I forget. I will always need to keep my tool kit within reach, working every day of my life, fixing the problems my mother and dad caused me. I will have courage. I will never allow the people to win who have treated me not as their equal, who thought of me as a failure because of my family circumstances. It has always been important for me to prove their opinion of me wrong.

I believe my strong desire to show evidence they misjudged me made me more competitive, steadfast, and gave me absolute determination. I guess you could say all these individuals who had decided my inadequacy, my weakness, and the wretched conclusion of my life helped make me successful. They never knew me. They never wanted to know me. But what they all thought they did know was how negligible my future.

I love Rosiclare; however, I will remember some people investing all in themselves. God gave me three elderly family members who loved me and believed in me. Their love would ultimately lead me to the good life. Those old people had nothing to offer but their love and their faith in Jesus.

When I became a wife and mother, I began to reflect, study, and consider my upbringing. I would deliberate and ponder over their life and their obedience and willingness to their core values. Mamaw, Pa, Aunt Lottie's intent was to nurture, guide, and inspire me to do good things with my life. Now, I made mistakes. I have not accomplished anything in my life that is deserving of any more recognition than you deserve in your life.

Reflecting on my life enabled me to assess and better understand my low self-confidence which would give me many limitations. I had the memory of my past. My protectors, those three old people who raised me. I had my warrior husband who loved, supported, and took care of the princess in the castle. My protectors and my warrior were holding tight to this defenseless little girl and wife. And soon now, I would become the woman to take a stand and defend myself and others when necessary. At last, I had arrived, and my arrival would continue for the remainder of my life.

I had no idea the day I accepted a position in the office for an insurance agency would be the start of a new beginning. I had been a licensed agent for a short period of time. One day, a field representative with a company the agency served visited the office. Mr. H handed me an insurance brochure introducing a new coverage and policy. He told me I had the personality to be a successful insurance policy sales agent. He said I could grow sales, and he asked me to try my success at selling this new product and his company to potential insureds. I had given no thought to sales. At that time, insurance salespeople were primarily men. Mr. H. believed in me. For some unknown reason, he had become aware and recognized something in me no one else was able to see. Just the fact he was recognizing me at all was a significant difference from what my life had been accustomed. I had to try. I could not disappoint him. I could not fail to meet his expectations and hope for me, the agency, and the company he represented. He was the only individual other than Gary and the people I talk about who considered my capabilities.

As always, Gary was supportive, providing me with encouragement. Gary was excited and gave me comfort, which motivated and strengthened my strong will. Gary was always there for me when I needed him. It did not matter how busy he was or how occupied he was with his career. He always had the time for me. God gave me Gary as my deposit to the start of a happy purposeful life. I would have a life of intention. I had a lot of things I wanted to achieve. I would aim high. My high aim was realistic, prudent, and relatively modest. Even though I was happy, even though I knew Jesus, I would always carry with me the pain of being abandoned. I would always wear the sadness of Rosiclare, extended family, and public school days on my person.

Some of my unflinching, unwavering, unshakable determination was a result of always needing to be worthy and accepted. I should have closed that chapter a long time ago. I never ended or detached myself from those early years of my life. I was not bitter toward them. I needed to remember. They were all a part of my past. Remembering kept me grounded and in complete control of my destiny. It kept me knowing what is to be valued in life. It allowed me to share with you my true and heartfelt story. To assure you making your life good can happen. Live the core values Mamaw taught. Align with people whose beliefs and actions are similar to yours. People who lift you up and encourage you. Build your relationship with the Lord. If you can manage this, you are on your way to great happenings.

I decided to try my luck at selling insurance. What did I have to lose? I was thirty-one years old, an office job with no future, and the job paid a very small salary. I began selling insurance on my lunch hour. To my surprise, I was becoming successful. I soon began to love selling. After a couple of years selling and many insureds, I was made a minority partner. There was only me and Mr. C. as partners and owners. I loved selling, and I worked hard. Most of my insureds were large commercial accounts. However, as a minority owner, I had no voice in any decision involving the agency. The same man who asked me to be a partner because he recognized my ability to sell and my devotion to my insureds was unable to ask or consider my advice or recommendation regarding agency matters. I had to make a decision.

As a minority owner and a growing book of business, I still was not making any money. God was there again. His plan for me was to start my own independent insurance agency. My decision was final. I would dissolve the partnership and go out on my own. I started my solely owned agency on October 1, 1983. Gary gave me his blessing and his full support of confidence. This decision would prove to be very advantageous for me and my family. Mamaw's wisdom, prudence, and discernment would divulge itself to me many times. Mamaw's teaching helped me make good business decisions. She taught honesty would always serve me best. Honest people have more courage, more confidence, and they speak the truth. Honest people are genuine. They do not pretend. A sure way to find trouble is to invite a dishonest person into your life. Individuals who are honest and have good character will honor their word. She taught keeping your word builds trust and credibility. She would always say to me, "You can lock your doors from a thief, but there is nothing you can do to a liar but always remove yourself from all association with them."

If we make a mistake, that does not make us a bad person. Everyone makes mistakes. Making mistakes is part of life. Good people learn from their mistakes. Good people will own and admit their mistakes and shortcomings. They will take responsibility for their words, behavior, or actions. And they will hold themselves accountable, focusing their time and energy on solving the problem they created. They will learn a valuable lesson. The lesson they will learn is not to make that mistake again.

Mamaw coached me to believe in myself. This took many years to acquire. She also coached me to not become overconfident, becoming arrogant and condescending. Be proud of who you are and the life you have been given. Never become so proud of yourself that you believe you are more deserving than others. Do not become self-centered and self-important. Stay free of pride but accept what you have accomplished with humility. Being wise is understanding and embarking on a personal relationship with humility.

As I have told you before, all there was to do growing up Rosiclare was build relationships. Mamaw and I had a loving relationship. She made sure it was also an understanding relationship. Her definition of this understanding relationship would be, she was the teacher and I was the student. This understanding relationship she insisted on was her show of unconditional love and devotion to me. She was facilitating my direction trying to eliminate many bumps and barriers leading to the good life. Human nature being what it is, I did not always comply with her teaching. And this action would result in presenting me with a problem I would have to solve.

Some people's life will grant them to always be able to ride the elevator. However, some of us will find it necessary to always climb the stairs, thus making life harder. From my beginning, it would be required of me to always climb the stairs. Nothing for me has been easy. My life started out empty with no one. Being denied the love and protection of my biological mother and dad. Given away by my parents at six months of age. I was disposed of by parents like you would throw away an old worn-out shoe. I was given to a soon-to-be widowed poor grandmother to raise. My elderly grandmother would wash and iron for people to support me. She would receive nothing from my parents to help care for me. Then came the contempt of my extended family. They were angered Mamaw was eliminating and relieving mother and dad of all responsibility and duty of me. Of course, there was the sadness and isolation I was made to feel all through Rosiclare Public Schools. My classmates saw me every day for twelve long years, but I was always unseen. My always present menace, Miss X, made certain I was bullied and intentionally made to feel unworthy of classmates' approval. Some classmates accommodated Miss X in fulfilling her wishes for making me feel undeserving of their friendship. Next came graduation, and I would leave the three old people I loved so much. Leaving Rosiclare was necessary, and I would be forced to ask for help from a second cousin I did not know. I am in Jacksonville, Illinois, a city of approximately 30,000 people then.

All my life I lived in Rosiclare with a population of 2,200 people. I had been outside the city limits of Rosiclare very, very few times my entire life. I walked everywhere I went. I recognized everyone I saw. I am in a strange place, 240 miles from home with only $50 in my pocketbook. I would find a secretarial job, little pay, and I would walk thirteen blocks to and from work for a total of nine months. I would at last be able, in March 1966, to buy a car. Now I could drive to work and I could drive to Rosiclare to visit Mamaw, Pa, and Aunt

Lottie. I could also see my best friend Carole and her parents whom I also missed very much. I worked at the same job for three and a half years. I lived alone in one room all that time.

But God had a marvelous plan waiting for me. The young man I loved, admired, and respected, the young man I had been patient and waited on for more than three years, was now proposing marriage. Gary and I were married January 26, 1969. I would not have many stairs to climb of several years. God stayed with me, watching me climb my past stairs. He was making sure I did not fall so hard as to harm his plan for my life, a plan God had for me since before I was ever born. He was teaching me to face adversity with courage and resilience. I came to learn with Mamaw's loving arms always outstretched to receive me; Gary as my supportive, kind, compassionate loving husband, and God holding me close and promising to never abandon me, I now experienced no fear. The confidence, the courage my Mamaw instilled in me and took years to gradually establish had been achieved. I am loved, happy, and probably for the first time in my life, I know I am equal to everyone.

Had I fallen down the stairs and not got back up, my life and future would have most likely been considered a failure. I had been given a strong willpower. God allowed my life to be burdensome, assuring I would stay strong. Remembering and never forgetting is important. We are not holding onto the past. We are saving the good and the bad memories. Our past will keep in check and balance our future. No matter how hard or painful our past, we refuse to self-destruct wallowing in pity. Instead we know what we must do for a good life. We must continue to climb the stairs. We must put into use every day Mamaw's constant command, her directive, her life compass which was, "NEVER QUIT—NEVER GIVE UP."

I was about to start a long, challenging, much hard work and effort to climb. This flight of stairs would require much determination, perseverance, dedication, and tenacity. It would also require the patience and understanding of Gary and our two girls. This climb would require toughness. The mounting difficulties would skyrocket. There were days when all I had was problems. But I stayed the course and kept ascending those stairs. I held on, I kept on, I persisted on, I continued on, I pressed on, I endured on, I climbed one step at a time very slowly, and I made the climb. I had been in a fierce battle with a long flight of steep stairs. I was the winner. I had beaten all the odds. These stairs represented my independent insurance agency. The agency was a success. I sold the agency and retired on October 1, 2016, after thirty-three years.

I am ready to start climbing the stairs once again. I began this new business with no money, no contract with an insurance company to represent. I had nothing to sell. It was not going to be easy finding an insurance company who would believe in me and give me a chance to prove myself. In 1983, insurance agency owners were primarily men. I was a female, no insureds and no policies to show them. I had to leave all the insureds and the policies I had sold at the old agency. I would not be able to take them with me until they renewed. Even then it would be necessary for me to sell them all over again. How the insurance industry works is all the policies I sold in the past would be renewed and given to my old agency.

I am positive a lot of people thought my new business of becoming an independent insurance agency owner would fail. I was told this by some old-fashioned negative fussy men. They gave me some reasons for what they believed would be the collapse of my agency. They told me I would not be able to keep the agency. They told me success was not in my future. Most all insurance agencies had partners and producers. I would be alone. I would be the only owner, only producer, and would have no employees for almost a year. To complicate matters, I had zero money. Gary's career had recently taken off at Duke. We had left the Navy eleven years earlier making just enough money to survive. Gary started at the bottom with Duke Energy. The jobs I had paid me a miserable salary. After paying the daycare for our little girls, there was very little left of my meager paycheck. Gary and I had a mortgage and a car payment, and all the other household expenses. We also had the comfort, security, and the future of two little girls to think about and plan. Our financial responsibility was not greater than most families. We did not waste our income on an extravagant and thriftless lifestyle. And now regardless of how small it was, I would be bringing no earnings to our household. It was difficult to save much money at that particular time in our married life.

I was going to need money to operate the new agency. I had left Gary to pay all of the expenses for our family and I was not going to ask him to fund and support my new business venture. Gary was supportive and allowed me to manage this idea of becoming an agency owner on my own. He would give me his suggestions and advice only if I asked. He never tried to tell me how to organize, direct, or run my agency. And in thirty-three years of being in business for myself, Gary's actions toward the agency never changed. He would tell me often he was proud of me and my performance in the agency. Gary knew me better than I knew myself. He was convinced of my success. He believed in me long before I believed in myself. I was able to deliver on his belief in me. Having Gary's support and faith sustained me for thirty-three years in the agency. God was the biggest contributor to the success I was about to experience. Regarding the agency, I always considered my success to be the following: (1) Making the companies I represented happy and money. Without them, I have nothing to sell and I am out of business. They would take their contract if I did not show to them a profit.

(2) I would provide to my insureds support in all areas of selling and servicing their policy. My obligation to my insureds stayed strong and professional. I was there to offer help and solutions to all their insurance concerns. Once I made the decision to sell an insured a policy, my first priority was no longer the company I represented. It now belonged to my insured for as long as I was their agent. These insureds had given to me their trust, confidence, and their respect.

I had taken many of these business insureds from agencies who had insured them for several years. Some of them had been with the same agency many years. I was dedicated, focused, and committed to taking care of their insurance needs. My insureds and I enjoyed a comfortable and pleasant working relationship with mutual trust and respect. I would not disappoint them. I appreciated them, and I thanked them from the bottom of my heart. My insureds had given me their business, their loyalty, and their friendship. They all knew it would be a fighting chance, but they gave me a chance to do what I loved. I loved selling and servicing insureds. I will always remember them and be humbled by the opportunity they granted me. They all had no idea of the help they were to me in building my confidence and making me feel worthy of their acceptance.

(3) The remainder of my goal for the agency was to make Gary and the girls proud. I wanted to have fun, and I wanted to make a little money. I believe I was successful in completing all of these objectives. I am only sharing my story of success with you because I want you to have a good and successful life too. I was raised poor. I was not a good student, and I was not a smart student. I rarely made a school grade higher than a C. I had no personality, and my life story had been one of rejection. But I remembered so many things my Mamaw told me. She always told me work would give my life purpose and meaning. This is so true. God will give you direction and give you all you need in health and talent. However, God will not do the job for you. Let me be clear, he will not do the work, make the sacrifice, and climb the stairs for you. But he will be your guide and give you success in all things if you let him. Remember too, success is not all about making money. For me, it was making my family proud, taking care of my insureds, and making Mamaw's dream for my life come to fruition. It was thanking God for his love and grace and giving him all the glory for my life and accomplishments.

I launched into my new business venture, renting a one-room office. I bought a used desk and chair. I purchased a used typewriter and copier. Everything I secured for the agency was secondhand. The copier was so old it took ink toner. Every print the copier made would leave my hands stained with toner. A local bank would loan me $5,000 for ninety days. I would pay it back in eighty-eight days and borrow the $5,000 again on the ninety-second day. This same banking transaction and banking relationship happened over and over. For months I would go to my filing cabinet and find only two homeowner policies. I was afraid of failing and maybe putting my family in debt. I did not want to let down all those business owners who trusted me with insuring their livelihood. I was insistent on satisfying the expectations of my family and others who gave me a chance.

I had already conquered the first step and possibly the most difficult. I had gone out on my own. Even though I had the belief and the reliance of Gary, I knew this enormous endeavor of success or failure sat on my shoulder alone. I never thought of giving up. I never thought of quitting. I only thought of reaching my goal. I promised myself I would work hard and do my best. I would thank God for this opportunity. I would thank him for every win regardless of how small.

I have been in business for a few years. I was no longer afraid of the agency failing. I worked hard, I kept my word, and I made prudent business decisions. I loved selling and servicing my insureds. My love of the insurance industry was not a job but my career. This was my calling, my God-given talent. This was part of my life's plan. I knew insurance, and I would explain coverages to insureds in such a way they were easily understood. Insurance is difficult to comprehend. I wanted each of my insureds to have a deep level of knowing their coverages.

I also loved the competition. I loved helping people protect their family and their business. I never was concerned about the money. Remember I have always been a low-maintenance woman. I learned as a youth what to value in life. All the teaching, instruction, and examples of Mamaw had resonated. I was reminded every day in my agency of her wisdom, strength, courage, and integrity. All those years growing up Rosiclare, I had been watching and studying.

Mamaw made me aware of what to do. More importantly, I learned from her what not to do.

I walked all over town in three-inch heels selling insurance policies. The agency grew to be very successful with 85 percent of my insureds being commercial accounts. I owned the agency from 1983 to 2016, a total of thirty-three years to the day. From the very beginning, I wanted to do a good job. I wanted the agency to survive. I was able to move a lot of policies and premiums across my desk. I had been held close beginning as an infant who came into the world with no one. A girl who was shy and had no confidence until now. A girl who was only average in school. God had now presented this once shy girl with the gift of gab, determination, perseverance, and tenacity. I now had been made to have courage. I had been given Gary. I had been given a service-driven nature which proved me well in the agency. I had been coached, counseled, educated, groomed, guided, influenced, and taught life's most valuable lessons. This was all the result of God giving me a grandmother by the name of Carmel. This wise grandmother showed me love is more than a feeling of the heart. Love is doing something. Love is action.

God told me of his plan for my life. My assurance and my promise from him was never to be abandoned again. He told me it would be necessary for me to always climb the stairs. He made sure the words of Mamaw were heard daily. Her words of courage to always keep one foot in front of the other. Go forward and never turn back when the impossible is looking probable. Mamaw's words of "You are stronger than you think." He who was the giver of all the many blessings of my life. He who has steered me onto his right path when I veered off into a troubling direction. He who put all the wonderful people in my life; the people I have devoted a chapter. He put some not-so-nice people in my life too. He knew they were necessary for me to live the plan he perfected for my life. His love, his faithfulness, and his holding close my once-empty life can only be explained this way, "because that is who he is." God is love. Everything I have been given is a gift from him. God wanted me to have a good life. I wanted to have a good life. God was continuing with much patience in planning my life giving me much love, family, happiness, and purpose. I recognize you, God, as being the sole giver. Me and the people I love give you all the glory, praise, and honor.

I had grown to have a lot of confidence in my sales ability. I now thought of being such a good persuader of closing sales, I could sell ice cubes in Alaska. I thought I could sell a cup of steaming hot coffee in the Arizona desert. Gee, I had come a long way since Rosiclare! I was at last a member of the positive thinking class. Positive thinking will get things accomplished. Wishful thinking is waiting on someone else to get things done. This will rarely happen. Experience has shown me if you want something, it is necessary you go and get it. Even though my confidence seemed to soar, I never forgot my roots. I never became arrogant. In the agency and all through my life, I believed in getting the job done. But I am not concerned with getting the credit and recognition. My life's goal has always been to do a good job and be of service to family and work.

I remained faithful for thirty-three years giving professional, dedicated attention, and insurance help, assistance, and solutions beyond my contractual obligations to my insureds. I let them know I was grateful for their business. I was happy, positive, and I was genuine. I communicated well. I knew my competition's sales techniques. I knew when to walk away. I did my work with passion, investing my heart and soul. I stayed committed to achieving my ambition and my objective. My enthusiasm and my honesty for wanting the insurance needs of my insureds satisfied was obvious. It was apparent to all I loved my job, and I understood the seriousness of my obligation. My overarching service commitment to my insureds built lasting relationships, friendships, respect, and years of loyalty. That was the reason for my success. That is what set me apart from some other insurance agencies. I had my agency because I was forced to climb the stairs. I know several people who have an agency and were able to take the elevator. Anything I had was more than I had ever known. I learned to appreciate the little things. Success does not happen to most of us overnight. It is most always achieved inches by inches. Requires lots of long hard work. It requires knowing the good choices from the bad choices. It requires having the character to make the good choice when the bad choice appears easier and attractive.

My employees and my insureds actually built the greatness of my agency. They contributed more to my success than did I. I was very fortunate to have good employees. I went beyond to encourage and inspire my staff to do their best work and to develop their strengths. I listened to and considered their suggestions. Even though I had a successful business with loyal staff and insureds, I still did not have a real friend. I do well in a work environment. However, even today I still do not run a good race in winning friends. I still fail at establishing relationships. Still haunted by those sudden pangs of anguish growing up Rosiclare. A little now forgotten mining town. But in the 1950s and 1960s, a little southern Illinois town with an intimate connection to haughtiness. And a strong dominant sense of superiority to a widowed poor grandmother raising a granddaughter. A granddaughter whose both mother and dad gave away as an infant.

When these old hurts surface, a person has two choices. They can succumb to their deep feelings of inferiority and not oppose these disruptive emotions. They put into exertion their parents' lack of love and disregard for all areas of their life, destroying and shattering their well-being. They can yield to the failure that has been expected, decided, and deliberately preconceived by some cruel individuals. Or they will resist and be determined to prove with evidence of their success consisting of happiness and prosperity. They will not permit the emotional pain of being treated as unwanted, unworthy, and unaccepted to prevent them from making and living a good life. They will claim their strength, courage, and power. Forgiving releases and heals most all the pain. Remember your past with the loneliness and ostracizing directed to you for nothing you had done. But do not be a prisoner to those old wounds. Do not cling to your past. Now that you have overcome, be thankful. You have defeated your past sorrows to be remembered but never to be lived again. Your past made you who you are today.

I retired and sold the agency in 2016. The agency did much for me. It helped provide more financial security for my family. It gave me years of pleasure in servicing my insureds and providing financial stability for my staff. I loved the competition and the day-to-day challenges. The challenges were all workable, resolvable, and I learned a great deal from them. The agency revealed to Mamaw, Pa, Aunt Lottie, Carole, Hazel, and Harold they had been right about me. The little girl they loved and nurtured to adulthood was paying attention. They could all be proud and take credit for the good life I came to know. But without a doubt, the agency positively showed the unique ways of my identity. I knew who I was. I liked myself, I am proud to know I am indefatigable, assiduous, inquisitive, meticulous, and principled. But most of all, the agency gave me conviction God's close hold on my once-empty life. My life had done a 180-degree turnaround. I was in a lot of ways no longer the girl Gary married. He did not care, and he loved the change. Gary was everything I hoped for and dreamed of in a husband. His love, support, faithfulness, protection, and leadership to me and our girls sustained me all our married life. He is and always will be my prince charming.

A happy, purposeful life, and career is being consistent in your beliefs and principles. Your attitude and your personal business actions are anchored in core values. Your being happy is your responsibility. Remain humble and make your associates and colleagues individuals who will counsel you in wisdom. Be a person who needs and wants little. Be someone who seeks or demands no attention, no special privilege, or accolade. Look for ways to serve others and do not look for ways others can serve you. Helping people will raise them up and will give you a real and positive change in your life.

We will provide the help we can to stop a bad situation and hopefully show a solution. Sometimes we were given no help. But everyone sometime will be given help. If not for the help we received, our life would be lived out the way it began. A life forgotten. When you help someone, you make them feel important. Our parents and some others along our way tried to convince us of our insignificance. However, there will always be people in our life who will show us different. We have been helped and served well. We experience the difference this made in our life. We are obligated to help those in need.

I am still climbing the stairs. It is March 2021, and Mother is eighty-eight years old. She lives in Illinois by herself. Until now she was doing alright. We had a lady who was a family friend check on her daily. I lived ten hours away in South Carolina. However, I had been calling her every day for the last year or longer. Before Gary passed away in 2019, we were driving to Illinois every three months to see her and do things for her which needed our help. She was becoming very feeble. Her physical strength was concerning. We noticed the changes to her aged and frail little body. Mother was always brassy, sassy, and independent, but she could never be contented living alone. She was becoming increasingly dependent and the family witnessed she was getting to the place in her life for changes to be made. However, she did not want to leave her home and friends. Mother had suffered a couple of hard falls. Her aging body was physically weak. She struggled walking. But in March 2021 she experienced a life-changing hardship. She had a stroke. In addition to weakening her already feeble physical strength, the stroke damaged her eyesight. She could no longer take care of herself.

I was all the family mother had. Her only other children, a girl and a boy, by her second marriage were deceased. Had they been living, both would not have helped her, nor would they have been able to help her. Both their lives were sad and without hope. The truth is, they were a product of their upbringing. They did not use their bad upbringing as a reason to do better.

I made the decision to bring mother to South Carolina to live with me. I did not do this because I wanted to. I did it because she was my mother and she needed help. No one was available but me. I also did this because she was Mamaw's daughter. Mamaw loved her and would want me to see she was cared for in every possible way. I had forgiven her a long time ago. Mother for the first time was no longer verbally abusive. She was now dependent, frail, almost blind, and being cared for by her first child. The child she gave away as a baby.

Mine and Gary's two daughters helped me a lot with mother. We all live in the same town. It is now July 2022, and I am one month from seventy-five years old. By this time, mother's dementia was progressing at a rapid pace. I had done everything for my mother since bringing her to live with me. This had always been an arduous challenge for me. All my time of twenty-four hours a day, every day, consisted of caring for her. The job of caring for her was wearing on my physical health. Caring and meeting her every need was hard labor, strenuous, and exhausting. It involved a lot of effort both mental and physical. I deliberated, gave careful thought, discussed with my daughters, and prayed about putting my mother in an assisted living facility. I was very kind, caring, and good to her my entire life but especially the time she lived with me.

Truthfully, I never gave any thought to the question of my love for her. However, I found the answer to that question the day I had to leave her at the assisted living home. I learned I did love her. I cried and cried. It broke my heart. The assisted living facility was nice and it was local. I went every day to see her. She loved chocolate ice cream. Every day I would take her chocolate ice cream or a chocolate milkshake. Both girls, her granddaughters, visited her three or four times a week. Mother had lots of family for company. Unfortunately, she was not able to enjoy our visits. Her health and mind kept her from caring or knowing we came to see her because we loved her. But the girls and I knew we were there. Mother passed away several months later while at the assisted living facility. Her doctors had conveyed to us there was no more they could do to help her. My mother's life was sad. For some unknown reason, she was never able to be happy. But I do know the last couple of years of her life she made her acquaintance with peace.

I think I have almost finished my climb. I may have reached the top of my lifelong climb up those frightening steep stairs. Sometimes I fell down, but I always got up. What an exhilarating finish to that long and gradual flight of stairs. My climb has been inspiring, invigorating, rewarding, problematic, and many eye-opening surprises delivering countless lessons learned.

I am looking back and carefully reflecting on and meditating on my life's now to be considered long journey. The people I donate a chapter gave me my attitude, my thoughts, my desires, my wisdom, my work ethics, my dreams, and my motivation. Growing up, my grandmother did not allow me to have my way. She directed my steps, and she paved my path with the example of her Christian life. I realize now my grandmother's ambition was for me to know I was loved and wanted. Her ambition was never about greed; it was never about money. However, it was about her being successful. Mamaw's ambition was desiring, and striving to be worthy of the blessing God had presented to her. Her ambition never wished for praise, an award, or a promotion. Her ambition was always focused on assuring she was following God's plan. The blessing she had been given was the responsibility of raising this little grandchild. And her ambition was for me. Raising me was a huge sacrifice for Mamaw. For eighteen years all my needs were met, and I remember her seldom doing or receiving anything for herself. Raising me was also a big risk. My grandmother had courage. She would embrace this challenge with hopefulness and joy.

For eighteen years, it would be necessary for her to be constantly physically exhausted from all those washing and ironings, making $20 a week. She would always only have just enough money for bare necessities. Most people would consider her life inadequate. But because of her love for me, her desires and ambition for me, she was happy with the struggle. She knew her own strength. She would never be given help of any kind from mother and dad regarding my well-being. My parents never cared about the hardship my grandmother faced every day providing for their little girl. I was their responsibility. But they disposed of me like you rid yourself of junk, scrap, and clutter. My parents would never find a place for me in their heart and conscience. They never heard that inner voice from God he generously speaks to all. Mother and dad were showing pieces of who they were. They had defined their values and I was not one of them.

I have said my grandmother's ambition was never for praise, award, or a promotion. I am certain she has been given an official award of the highest honor for her success, devotion, difficult struggle, and completion of God's plan. This official Hero's award in recognition of years of gallantry, sacrifice, faith, and prayer has been presented to my grandmother by Jesus Christ. Her outstretched arms were always there to hold me when I was growing up Rosiclare. And I ran into those loving arms many times throughout my life. Her arms were always open to receive me, console me, comfort me supplying my every need. I never had to worry about Mamaw's arms closing or being crossed. I never had to worry about her abandoning me. This grandmother always loved me unconditionally. One day I will run to her arms again. I am assured her arms will be outstretched waiting to receive me.

There have been times I failed Mamaw, Pa, Aunt Lottie, Carole, Hazel, and Harold. But they never failed me. God made me meek so I would obey. He allowed me to be poor in my youth so I would share with others what I had been given in my adult years. He gave me courage to carry on with strength of mind and body because he had a plan for me already in the making. He gave me wisdom so I would turn to him for help and direction. God let me understand little is big if he is in it!

I do not know if God has more stairs for me to climb. If he does, with his blessing I will climb them and reach the top. My life has been good. It was made better because I was made to take the stairs. I never ask for much. Only to be loved and accepted. But instead, God gave me everything. Most importantly, by the giving of his grace, I know Jesus Christ as my Savior. We are constant companions.

My life is better than my favorite fairy tale, Cinderella. My fairy tale is real.

> "For I know the plans I have for you," declares the Lord, "Plans to prosper you and not harm you, plans to give you hope and a future." (Jeremiah 29:11 KJV)

Me, August 1950 at home in Rosiclare.

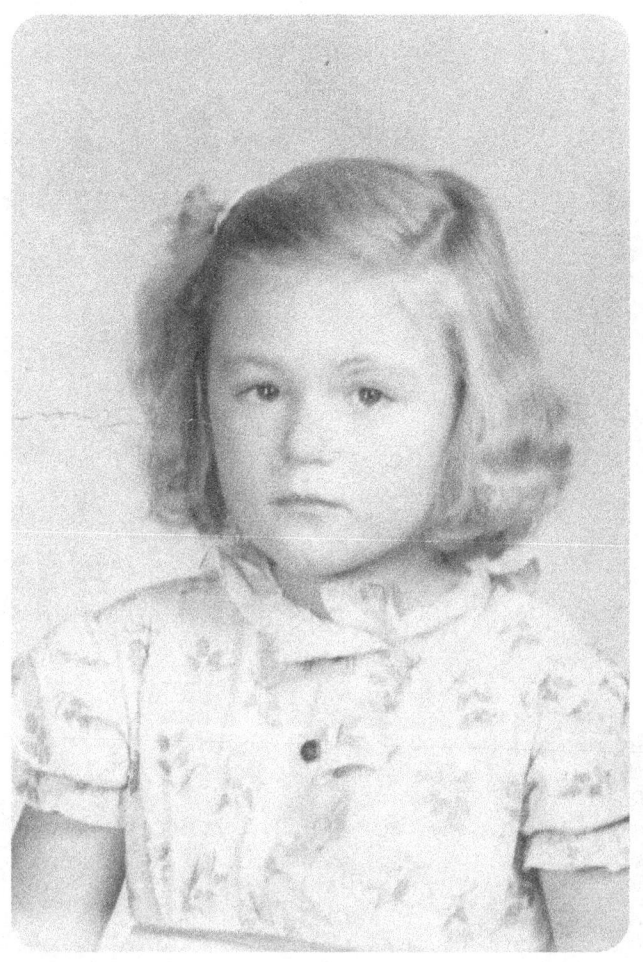

Me in second grade at Rosiclare school.

My Rosiclare High School Graduation Portrait.

Me and daughters, Stephanie and Stacy.

My young family.

One of God's many blessings, my family.

All grown up. So proud of my family.

16

Because of God, Mamaw, and My Life Makers

It has been difficult for me to share my story with you because it is so personal. I have always been humble and do not require attention. This book is straight from my heart. I wrote this book because both my parents gave me away as an infant. I know the problems this action brings to a young child's life. The trauma of being abandoned by mother and dad is the same for all of us. We just cope and manage the best we can. I know God has laid on my heart to share with you my story. This book was written with two motives. The most important is to share his love for you. I hope you will have the desire to be a good Christian. The second motive for this book tells you the good life can be yours.

I am proof a life born to emptiness can become a life blessed beyond expectation. Proof your life story does not need to be the same narrative as your beginning. Both my parents brought me into this world with no hope. For reasons I started life with a great disadvantage. A life most people thought of as unfavorable with a restricted chance for happiness and success, a life with no vision, a life without purpose, but God had a plan.

You have discovered by now I am no wordsmith. Just a very simple girl who learned at an early age what was important. To appreciate the little things. A girl who unfortunately still today must prove first to herself and then to those old foes she is their equal. A simple girl born and raised in a small now-forgotten mining town in Southern Illinois. Raised by three elderly extended family members who owned nothing but their integrity. I was not intended to be their responsibility. They took me, they loved me, and they wanted me.

I was left at the mercy of a grandmother, Carmel. This aging, poor, widowed Mamaw had nothing but love, and devotion to give me. She gave and kept her love strong, loyal, and alive for me beginning to end. Mamaw and I walked to church for years. She took me to church beginning at a very young age. Her most important assignment for me was to know Jesus. Because of Mamaw, I was introduced to Jesus Christ.

The window to my life those three elderly extended family members offered me looked limited. However, this offering has sustained me all through my life without interruption. This offering of what appeared to be a limited window seeing my future. It took me years to realize this window to my future I thought was small was factually huge. It was watching them live their life by example. Always for me to observe and learn their discipline and obedience to their faith and their core values. The window I thought was limited granted to me everything needed for a purposeful life. They offered me all they had. They offered me opportunity. A future I would not know but for them. They handed me a testimony to share with you.

I never made the honor roll in school. At best, I was an average student. I had no friends except for Carole, no ambition, and no qualities that would be worthy of giving recognition. God gives his strongest in our lives when we are the weakest and the most frightened.

A young child weakened by the abandonment of my mother and dad. Feelings of insecurity and believing I was unworthy of being liked. But at twenty-one months of age, he put Carole, Hazel, and Harold in my every day.

They were with me some of every day of my life until I left home after high school graduation. They did not just like me. They loved me. I carry in my heart always their memory. They were inspiring me to believe in myself. They gave me much solace and support. They gave with enthusiasm interest in this little abandoned girl. I would come to realize all this was done because they loved me and wanted for me a good life. This has been validated by my need for and my use of lessons learned from their actions. A child remembering three lives whose kind hearts were motivated by and always held close by the Holy Spirit.

A shy and naive young girl on her own and scared. And then one day in 1965, Gary was introduced. He would be just what I needed for God's plan to continue. He was a man I would marry and love for the remainder of my life and longer. He was what every young girl yearns for and hopes to find. Gary was kind and smart, had good work ethics, and exhibited Mamaw's core values. He supported and believed in me. There is no doubt my life has been made better because of Gary. Gary had the willingness to always put my happiness above his. His desire was to secure the well-being of me and the girls. Showering us with love and care. We would spend more than fifty wonderful years together. He made me complete. With Gary's passing, my life seems vacant. He always made sure the girls and I knew we were his high priority.

A good man giving perfect love to a once-abandoned and forgotten little girl. Gary lived his life far and beyond. In every aspect of his life, he gave more human decency and more goodwill than anyone would expect. Anyone who knew Gary would agree this defines him.

My young life, to some people, was dull and boring. You have learned my young life might be considered incredibly uninteresting and monotonous. It was a life no one would dream of experiencing. A young girl whose personality content was comprised of unstimulating and unattractive marks of description. My personality growing up was quiet, shy, and stale. I was verified and confirmed by some members of my extended family, classmates, church members, and some of Rosiclare's elitists to be unacceptable and unimportant. But I was given seven life makers who knew different.

The good people I donate a chapter were given a big assignment. This job assignment was being my life makers. They all had the necessary qualifications to perform this huge task. A task given to their heart by the one in authority. My longing and desire for a good life was cemented by them. All seven of them carved for me a road to learn, grow, and reach my potential. They helped me identify my talents and strengths. They made me want to hold my head high.

There is no such thing as life without setbacks and challenges. There will always be someone or something going over the line and getting in our lane. Every dream that is fought for, lived, and accomplished is done by taking control of and conquering trouble. Never give up on yourself. Never give up on your goals. Never give up on living the good life.

If you fail, you will learn from your mistakes. If you succeed, you will triumph. But if you give up, if you quit, you are being defeated by emotion. This action will leave you lost, hollow, and idle. Be determined and remember the words of my wise Mamaw, "NEVER QUIT—NEVER GIVE UP."

I believe I was supposed to share my story that will assuredly have many life similarities to those of you abandoned as infants or young children. People treating us with indifference because we were abandoned by our parents. These people would be so arrogant and condescending they could not see we were already wounded by the show of no concern, no interest, no care, from mother and dad. Certain individuals' unpleasant attitude toward us gave no reasoning other than their feeling of superiority.

I hope my sharing with you many of my insecurities and sufferings caused me by my abandonment will give you hope and determination. This book detailing my life is meant to inspire you to create attainable goals and pursue them to fruition. You can live the realization of your dreams if they are realistic and possible to achieve. Necessary for success includes hard work, discipline, and persistence. You can awaken every day to a good life.

There is a plan for your life. A good plan for you designed by the greatest of architects, and it is sealed with your name. Pray and ask God to show and prepare you for his plan. I believe prayer is to God what energy is to us. The right prayer, the right timing, the constant prayer, I believe, has the same results with God as energy, hard work, and tenacity have with us. Never give up on God's faithfulness. Be patient for his plan is always working for your life. However, he is working on his time schedule, not yours. Remember too, he is never late, never early, but always on time.

Success holds a lot of interpretation. The greatest definition of success is having a personal relationship with Jesus. He is the thread that holds the fabric of life together. The spotlight of our attention needs to stay focused on him.

I hope you have life makers. I hope your love and faith in God will grow stronger with each passing day. Your Christian life has a beginning, but it has no end.

> But they that wait upon the Lord shall renew their strength; they shall mount up with wings as eagles; they shall run, and not be weary; and they shall walk, and not faint. (Isaiah 40:31 KJV)

Conducting God's plan, you can have a life of love, happiness, peace, and enlargement—a life of enriching days and years. Always let your biggest success be your personal relationship with Jesus Christ. Give to him all the glory.

Mamaw, Carmel, had a strong working relationship with God. Strong faith gave sight to her finished task of raising me. She saw the result of this big job God had directed her before it became a visible reality. I have done nothing to deserve the blessings God has given to me. Because a loving God placed this little six-month-old baby in the arms of a devoted grandmother, my empty life was saved. A baby brought into this world empty with no one. But God had a plan, and he will NEVER QUIT—NEVER GIVE UP. God is never-ending love.

Oldest daughter, Stephanie's Wedding, June 1994.

Daughter, Stacy's Wedding, March 2002.

My best friend Carole, her dear husband Roger, and
my Gary are God's gifts of his love to me.

Marlene grew up in a good, God-fearing family with a grand-mother, great-aunt, and great-grandfather. She was tremendously loved by these three people—especially her grandmother.

I never knew nor met her father—he was never there!

Her mother was another story—seldom around, and one was glad to see her go when she left. Why—because her mother cursed God, her grandmother, and anyone else who crossed her path. I feel the mother led a very sad life, and I hope she made peace with our heavenly Father before she passed from this life.

Susie
Rosiclare, Illinois

About the Author

The author was born and raised in the small Southern Illinois town of Rosiclare. At six months old, she was abandoned by both parents and given to a poor widowed grandmother to raise. She learned life was not about her roots commencing in poverty, lacking money to live at a quality level considered normal and acceptable in society. She would realize, too, that life was not about her knowing parents did not want her. But life is about what she would do with what she had been given.

She was the sole owner of a successful independent insurance agency for thirty-three years. She was on the Agents Advisory Council, Southeastern Region, for one of the large insurance companies her agency represented. The author has organized and been master of ceremonies for many fundraisers. She has been the president of a women's club, showing herself to be an unrelenting, decisive, and inspiring leader.

She and her husband have two daughters and three grandchildren.

I cannot think of my childhood without thinking of Marlene. We were inseparable. Marlene was raised by her grandmother, Pa (which is what the neighborhood kids called him), and Aunt Lottie (again she was everybody's aunt).

There was so much love in that home except when Marlene's biological mother came to visit. Everyone knew that the results of her visit, no matter how long she stayed, would end in chaos. Marlene's mother was very critical and condescending to Marlene and her grandmother. Sometimes the visit would only last less than an hour because she would show her nasty side and leave.

As the years go by, Marlene showed the forgiveness and love that she had for her mother regardless of how she was abandoned by her as a child. She moved her mother to her home, provided for her, and made her last days here on earth as comfortable as possible.

Marelene's dad was always absent. He never made himself present in her life.

Carole
Rosiclare, Illinois

215